TALES FROM THE
DUKE BLUE DEVILS
LOCKER ROOM

TALES FROM THE
DUKE BLUE DEVILS
LOCKER ROOM

A COLLECTION OF THE GREATEST
DUKE BASKETBALL STORIES EVER TOLD

JIM SUMNER

SPORTS
PUBLISHING

Visit our website at www.sportspubbooks.com

10 9 8 7 6 5 4 3 2 1

Library of Congress Cataloging-in-Publication Data is available on file.

ISBN: 978-1-61321-053-6

Printed in the United States of America

CONTENTS

ACKNOWLEDGMENTS

Writing and talking about Duke basketball is a labor of love for me. Making it easier was a large group of people who helped facilitate this project. Thanks to Jon Jackson and Paulette Rogers of Duke University sports information, Pam Matheson and Mary Dinkins of the Duke Varsity Club, and the staffs of Duke University Archives, North Carolina State Archives, and the North Carolina State Library.

Most of all, my wife, Ann, whose patience seems to be inexhaustible.

The majority of this book was taken from interviews with the following people who shared their time and memories: Mark Alarie, Bucky Allen, Tate Armstrong, Gene Banks, Joe Belmont, Jay Bilas, Bob Bradley, Robert Brickey, Vic Bubas, Tom Butters, Jeff Capel, Terry Chili, Matt Christensen, Marty Clark, Hayes Clement, Johnny Dawkins, Rudy D'Emilio, Kenny Dennard, Randy Denton, Tony Drago, Danny Ferry, Bill Foster, Mike Gminski, Bob Harris, Bobby Joe Harris, David Henderson, Art Heyman, Grant Hill, John Hoffman, Carl James, Bernie Janicki, Billy King, Ed Koffenberger, Greg Koubek, Mike Lewis, Jack Marin, Ronnie Mayer, Dan Meagher, Gary Melchionni, Jeff Mullins, John Seward, Fred Shabel, Jim Spanarkel, Kevin Strickland, Jim Suddath, Bucky Waters, and Robby West.

The interviews listed in the acknowledgments section comprised the bulk of the stories told. Also consulted were the following newspapers: *The Charlotte Observer*, *The* (Duke) *Chronicle*, *Durham Morning Herald*, *Greensboro Daily News*, *The New York Times*, *The* (Raleigh) *News and Observer*.

Also consulted were the following books:

Barton, Don and Bob Fulton. *Frank McGuire: The Life and Times of a Basketball Legend*. Columbia, South Carolina. Summerhouse Press, 1995.

Brill, Bill. *One Hundred Seasons. Duke Basketball: A Legacy of Achievement*. Champaign, Ill. Sports Publishing, 2004.

Groat, Dick, with Frank Dascenzo. *I Hit and I Ran*. Durham, N.C. Moore Publishing Company, 1978.

Krzyzewski, Mike, with Donald Philips. *Five-Point Play*. New York: Warner Books, 2001.

Landwehr, Hazel. *Home Court: Fifty Years of Cameron Indoor Stadium*. Winston-Salem, N.C. Hunter Publishing, 1989.

McKinney, Horace "Bones," and Garland Atkins. *Bones: Honk Your Horn if You Love Basketball*. Greensboro, N.C.: Garland Publishers, 1988.

Werber, Bill. *Circling the Bases*. Self-published. 1978.

TALES FROM THE
DUKE BLUE DEVILS
LOCKER ROOM

Chapter 1

SETTING THE STAGE

"CAP" CARD

Basketball was created by James Naismith, a New England physical education instructor. It is fitting that basketball was introduced at Trinity College by a New England-trained physical education professor.

Wilbur "Cap" Card graduated from Trinity College in 1900 and went north to Harvard, where he graduated from the Sargent Normal School of Physical Education in 1902. He came back to Trinity in 1902 to become director of physical education, a position he held until his retirement in 1948.

GETTING STARTED

"Cap" Card introduced basketball to Trinity College in January 1906. The school newspaper, *The Chronicle*, explained the new sport to the uninitiated on January 30.

It is well-nigh a certainty that Trinity is to have another game added to her list of athletic sports in the near future. The game in question is basket ball, one of the most fascinating and most intensely interesting indoor sports known today. Next to football it probably holds the constant attention of the spectators more than any other game. Anyone witnessing it will never forget it. The play is extremely fast and vigorous, yet open enough for an onlooker to follow the movement of the ball and the players…. In it a man of small stature has about an equal chance with a larger man; yet, of course an extremely quick, large man has somewhat of an advantage over an opponent of smaller size. Basket ball should appeal to a larger number of students than does base ball, for although it requires a great deal of skill, it is more readily adapted to unskilled players than is that game. Yet not everyone is a successful basket ball player, for everyone does not possess great activity, nerve and endurance, the three prime essentials of a good player.

THE FIRST GAME

After just few weeks of practicing, Trinity decided to test its mettle against the outside world. The first intercollegiate game was played March 2, 1906, and the opponent was Wake Forest College. The game was played in the Angier B. Duke gym, a tiny facility, which measured only 32 feet by 50 feet. Wake Forest had more experience than Trinity and easily handled the less-experienced Trinity team 24-10. Wake led 18-3 at the half.

The Chronicle wrote, "Trinity's defeat was due largely to the inexperience of the team, this being the first intercollegiate basketball contest in which she has ever engaged. Lack of confidence on the part of the home team made itself very evident in the first half. The game was an unusually clean one from start to finish. Very few fouls were called, and roughness was rare."

H.E. SPENCE

One of the participants offered his assessment of the first game. Trinity's H.E. Spence wrote in the 1950s, "[I]t was very difficult to throw goals when your guard was tattooing your ribs with his elbow, bumping you with his hip, stepping on your toe or grabbing you by the belt. The only fouls which were certain to be called were when two men ganged up on one, or when a man put both arms around the man he was guarding. Otherwise, he could hold, push and pull all he pleased. There were few fouls called for hacking, tripping, blocking, charging or even cross-hipping."

GOING SLOW

Trinity maintained a low profile in basketball for two decades. "Cap" Card coached only 47 games in seven seasons before giving up the coaching position. Trinity's schedule included a handful of high schools and YMCA teams.

Card was replaced by a succession of coaches, 10 between 1913 and 1928. The opponents were all local. Trinity occasionally played teams from neighboring states but didn't play a team from out of its immediate geographic area until the 1920s. Trinity did win 20 games in 1917, against only four losses. However, nine of the wins were against YMCAs or athletic clubs.

NOT MUCH OF A RIVALRY

On January 24, 1920, Trinity played its first game against the University of North Carolina, located only eight miles to the west. The Duke–North Carolina series is widely regarded as college basketball's top rivalry, but the beginning of the rivalry was inauspicious. North Carolina won the game 36-25.

UNC went big time in college basketball well before Trinity, and the results of that decision are indicated in the record books. North Carolina dominated the Mid-Atlantic for much of the 1920s, including an undefeated season in 1924. Included in that dominance was a 16-game winning streak against Trinity/Duke.

THE BLUE DEVILS

Duke's athletic teams have a distinctive nickname, the "Blue Devils." The name does not have any religious origin. The Blue Devils were a French Alpine fighting unit in World War I, well known for their courage and fighting spirit. They toured the United States in 1917 and 1918, raising money for the war effort. Irving Berlin even wrote a song about them. In 1921 the school newspaper began arguing that the traditional nickname "Methodists" was too bland for a time already becoming known as the Roaring Twenties. They wanted something catchier, something more distinctive. The student body in the early 1920s contained numerous war veterans, who were quite familiar with the Blue Devils of France. After several years of debate, the nickname was adopted in 1923.

STEPPING UP

Trinity College became Duke University in 1924. A new gym, Card Gymnasium, was built for basketball. Most importantly, in 1928 Duke joined the Southern Conference, the dominant athletic conference in the South. University president William Few wanted Duke to excel in sports but in such a way that would "integrate the sports of youth with the whole program of the university." Few laid out the philosophy that would guide Duke basketball into the 21st century. The stage was set for Duke to join the world of big-time college basketball.

EDDIE CAMERON

Duke's first big-time basketball coach was 26-year-old Eddie Cameron. He came to Duke in 1926 as an assistant football coach. He would stay at the school in one capacity or another for almost 50 years. He took over the basketball program in the autumn of 1928.

GLOWING RECOMMENDATION

Eddie Cameron interviewed at Duke in the spring of 1925, shortly after graduating from Washington and Lee. That school's president, Henry Louis Smith, highly recommended Cameron.

"I regard him as exceptionally qualified to be a high-class coach and guide a gentleman's team in any high-class institution. Nothing dishonorable or doubtful in ethics, ideals, or practice of an athletic team will be countenanced or allowed by such a young leader."

BILL WERBER

Eddie Cameron inherited some first-rate talent when he became head basketball coach in 1928. At the top of the list was Bill Werber, a native of Maryland who had come to Duke to play baseball. Werber arrived at Duke when the school was in the middle of an ambitious construction boom. It created some problems, Werber would write:

I was expecting to find a tranquil green oasis, magnolia trees, lilac bushes, and ivy-covered walls. Instead Duke was a mess... woe betide the errant or hasty walker on a rainy day. His clothes spattered and wet, he

Eddie Cameron

suffered… misery by becoming mired in mud. Dormitory doors were innocent of hardware, so when the wind blew at night, which it frequently did, those doors would bang, bang, bang down one side of the corridor and up the other, never in unison. Sometimes this clatter would continue all night long. The riveters would start on the steel work at the crack of dawn. All this plus the heat, dust, noise, and confusion, was just too much. Harry [teammate Harry Councillor] and I almost decided to pack up and go home. Duke, in September, 1926, was a sorry looking place.

Werber thought it over and stayed. The baseball part worked out well for Werber. He was a standout infielder at Duke. After graduation he would play 11 seasons in the major leagues, leading the American League in stolen bases three times. Famed baseball scout Paul Krichell once said that Werber "had the best baseball legs I ever saw, including [Ty] Cobb." Werber put that speed and athleticism to work for the basketball team. He excelled as a scorer, defender, and ball handler and was a key part of Duke's early success in the Southern Conference. In 1930 Werber became Duke's first basketball All-American.

COACH AND STAR

Fortunately for Duke, the new coach and the star player hit it off right away. Bill Werber felt that Eddie Cameron was "well-developed mentally, low-key, but with unusually good judgment. The ball players liked him and wanted to work with him. We all loved him and would never let him down."

Cameron was equally complimentary toward his star.

"The best player I ever coached was Bill Werber. Bill was a real scrapper. Bill was a student of the game. He paid enormous attention to details, to movements of other players. He was never surprised in a game. If anything opened up between him and the basket, he'd drive like anything for it, knowing he'd either get fouled or score."

THAT'LL GET HIS ATTENTION

In the early 1930s Duke was preparing to play North Carolina. Concerned with UNC's big center "Tiny" Harper, Bill Werber and Harry Councillor practiced throwing a ball at the head of Duke center Joe Crosson, who would duck as the ball approached him. At the beginning of the game with UNC, Werber fired ball at Crosson's head. He ducked and the ball hit Harper flush in the face, temporarily stunning him. The big man was strangely passive the rest of game.

IMMEDIATE SUCCESS

Eddie Cameron had immediate success at Duke. His first team ended its regular season with a modest 9-7 mark but qualified for the Southern Conference Tournament. The Southern Conference had 23 teams in those days so a postseason tournament involving the top teams was the only rational way to determine a champion. The tournament was held in Atlanta.

Duke opened with a win over Alabama and followed with wins over North Carolina and Georgia. The team didn't have much depth, and the five starters played virtually the entire time. Duke ran out of gas in the finals against North Carolina State and fell 43-35.

Cameron ended the long drought against North Carolina. In fact, Cameron won six of his first seven games against UNC. For the first time, the rivalry really was a rivalry.

Cameron's second team put together an 18-2 mark, still one of the top winning percentages in school history. Unlike some pre-Cameron teams, this club compiled the mark against top-level intersectional competition. Duke's only losses were to Washington and Lee and Alabama, the latter in the Southern Conference Tournament finals. Bill Werber described his senior team as "a very aggressive and scrappy small group of young men who did not take the floor expecting to lose."

FIRST INTERSECTIONAL WIN

Before Eddie Cameron's arrival, most of Duke's opponents were local teams from North Carolina or surrounding Mid-Atlantic states. This began to change in the early 1930s. One of the first high-profile intersectional games played by Duke was a 1930 match against Loyola of Chicago. Loyola had gone 16-0 in 1929 and entered 1930 eastern tour with a 34-game winning streak. They suffered losses to Duquesne and Georgetown, followed by a one-point win over North Carolina.

Loyola impressed observers with their discipline and poise. One area writer noted, "When they cut the ball loose, there was a purpose.

None of their shots were wild chances. Their passes were deliberately aimed."

Most of their passes were aimed at their star center Charles Murphy. One contemporary account raved, "Charles Murphy, the elongated center of the Loyolans, easily the greatest performer to ever perform in the Duke gymnasium, was just about the whole show for the visiting team." Murphy scored 19 points, a stunning total for 1930. Duke's big man Joe Crosson answered Murphy basket for basket. The contest was tied several times after intermission, the last time at 22-22. Crosson scored three times inside to give Duke a 28-22 lead. Loyola cut the margin to 29-27, but a Crosson free throw sealed the game and made the final score 30-27. Crosson ended with 14 points. The big win propelled the 1930 Duke team to an 18-2 record.

"MOUSE" EDWARDS

Fred "Mouse" Edwards was fan favorite in the late 1930s. A natural comic, Edwards kept his teammates in stitches. Teammate John Hoffman describes him as a "strange-looking guy, always cutting up." The irrepressible Edwards spent much of the game talking to referees, scorekeepers, and opposing players. His best-known escapade occurred in 1938 against Florida. Driving to the basket, Edwards was stripped of the ball by a Florida defender. Nonetheless he continued toward the Duke goal.

"He kept his right hand moving up and down, in his best dribbling form," Hoffman recalls. "As he reached the goal, Edwards wrapped both hands around the imaginary ball and pitched it toward the basket. And then actor Fred stared in utter amazement as no ball went through the hoop."

The crowd went wild.

NEVER A DULL MOMENT

The 1938 Duke team was arguably the most exciting team in Eddie Cameron's tenure. Duke sports information director Ted Mann dubbed this group the "Never a Dull Moment" team. Cameron had to replace most of his key players from the previous year. He was faced with putting together a cohesive unit from football players Bob O'Mara and Fred "Mouse" Edwards, baseball player Fred "Dutch"

Bergman, second-year law student John Hoffman, and local boy Ed Swindell.

The 1938 season was the first year when they did hold a center jump after made baskets, but players had become accustomed to numerous brief breaks in the game. Now they had to learn how to pace themselves differently.

"It became difficult to play the whole game," Hoffman says. "Very few players could go the distance."

Duke was unusually erratic that season. A two-week period when they lost to Davidson 40-22 and turned around and beat the Kentucky Wildcats 52-28 was typical of that year. Duke hovered around .500 all season. One local writer noted, "Duke has well-earned the cognomen of the 'unpredictable.' The wisest and most conservative of the sports writers have thrown up their hands in despair in trying to solve Duke's performance."

After a season of on-again, off-again play, Duke jelled in time for the tournament. Duke opened with a 44-33 upset of North Carolina State and their star Connie Mack Berry, a future Chicago Bear. Duke trailed Maryland most of their semifinal match, but Edwards came up big down the stretch, and Duke pulled off another upset 35-32.

Duke had advanced to the Southern Conference Tournament finals in 1929, 1930, 1933, and 1934 but had come up short every time. They finally pulled off a title in 1938. Duke was as loose as the proverbial goose before the title game. Cameron noted that his guys "were having a gleeful time. I found them forming a chorus and doing pretty well."

Swindell scored 14 points, Edwards added a dozen, and Duke cruised to a 40-30 win over Clemson. For some reason the All-Tournament team was selected at halftime of the finals. Duke had no representative on the team. Cameron informed his players of this fact at halftime and added, "You can't win anything except championships, so you need to win that if you're going to get anything out of this." Duke already led 20-11 at the half. Suitably inspired, they scored the first eight points after intermission to break open the game.

Hoffman remains proud of Duke's first championship team.

"Duke was a football school then, but I think we helped give basketball some recognition," he explains. "We definitely helped start something."

NEW PLACE TO PLAY

On January 1, 1939, the undefeated, untied, and unscored upon Duke football team traveled to Pasadena to play the University of Southern California in the Rose Bowl. Duke lost a heartbreaker 7-3. What does this have to do with basketball? Well, Duke made enough money from the game to finally begin construction on a new basketball facility to replace tiny Card Gymnasium, which had been built in the 1920s.

The Indoor Stadium had been under consideration for years, but the Great Depression had made money tight so the facility remained only a dream through much of the 1930s. Supposedly Eddie Cameron drew up plans for a new facility on the back of a matchbox. The original plan called for 4,000 seats, then 5,000, and then 8,000. Some thought the latter total was overly ambitious. Horace Trumbauer was the Philadelphia-based architect who designed much of the new construction on the Duke campus in the 1920s. Hired for the Indoor Stadium project, Trumbauer argued, "I think the sittings for 8,000 people is rather liberal. Yale has in its new gymnasium a basket ball court for 1,600." Duke officials thought otherwise and wisely went for a larger facility. Construction was completed in less than one year at a cost of about $400,000. (By contrast, Raleigh's RBC Center, which opened in 1999 and hosts North Carolina State's home games, cost around $158 million.) Another football bowl game, the 1945 Sugar Bowl, gave Duke enough money to finish paying for the building. It was the largest basketball facility on the East Coast south of Philadelphia's Palestra.

DEDICATING THE STADIUM

The Duke Indoor Stadium opened on January 6, 1940, a bitterly cold Saturday. Opening ceremonies were scheduled for 8 p.m. Ironically, the keynote address was delivered by University of North Carolina dean Robert B. House, who represented the Southern Conference. Precisely at 8 p.m., as House and other dignitaries made their way to the podium, the Indoor Stadium was plunged into darkness. A blown fuse caused a 10-minute power outage. Earlier in the week, North Carolina State's Thompson Gymnasium had suffered a similar blackout during a game. Courtside observers waggishly speculated that the new arena wasn't willing to concede anything to existing facilities.

Observers were wowed by the new building. The lower bleacher level was reserved for students, a successful arrangement that continues to this day. The upper level consisted of reserved "theater seats." This was the first time Duke had reserved seats. No longer was it necessary for fans to sit through a freshman preliminary game in order to have good seats for the main event.

GLEN PRICE

The first game in the Indoor Stadium was between Duke and Princeton. Duke forward Glen Price scored the first points in the Indoor Stadium with a free throw. Moments later he followed with the first field goal, for a 3-0 Duke lead. Price went on to score 13 points as Duke defeated the visitors 36-27. In 1972 the Indoor Stadium was renamed for Eddie Cameron. It is regarded as one of the nation's top college basketball facilities. Duke has won more than 82 percent of the home games played since it opened.

THE DURHAM HIGH SCHOOL GANG

Durham High School is located only a few miles from the Duke campus. In the late 1930s Durham High School had one of the nation's top prep teams, winning 69 consecutive games. Duke allowed the team to play its home games on campus and set about recruiting as many of the teams' players as they could. Duke succeeded in bringing in Bob Gantt, Gordon Carver, and brothers Cedric and Garland Loftis. All became top players at Duke. One of their teammates was John Seward, a native of Newport News, Virginia.

"If there was a Durham boy open and I was open, I didn't get the ball," Seward remembers. "The Durham boy did. I got them in the locker room and said, 'I'm here to play basketball just like you. If I don't get the ball when I'm open, then I'm coming after you.' I started getting the ball."

"BONES" McKINNEY

Although Duke was able to successfully recruit many of the local boys, the Blue Devils lost the top player from the Durham High School team.

"I lived a block from the Duke campus, and like that Duke Blue Devil, I lived and died with their football team," Horace "Bones" McKinney explains. "As a kid I had sold drinks in the stands just to get a ticket to see their games. I had played basketball in the Duke gym and knew all the boys on the Duke team. If I was wearing anything but Duke blue when I walked past the Duke Chapel, I felt like Benedict Arnold."

Eddie Cameron wanted McKinney in the worst way, but North Carolina State convinced McKinney to defect to Raleigh. After World War II, McKinney transferred to the University of North Carolina and later played six seasons in the NBA before coaching Wake Forest to the 1962 Final Four.

CAMERON'S LAST SEASON

The 1941-1942 team certainly had its share of distractions to contend with. The 1941 Duke football team went undefeated and earned a bid to the Rose Bowl. On December 7 the Japanese attacked Pearl Harbor, propelling the United States into World War II. The Rose Bowl was canceled and then rescheduled for Duke's campus. Eddie Cameron, still an assistant football coach, had to juggle both sports, while star center Bob Gantt's football obligations largely kept him off the hardcourt until January.

Gantt's absence was partially responsible for a 57-41 loss to Temple in the third game of the season. Duke then reeled off a 13-game winning streak. George Washington ended the streak with a 55-53 win, but Duke finished the regular season with three more wins, including a 41-40 nailbiter over UNC in Cameron's last home game.

Duke finished the season in fine style, defeating Washington and Lee 59-41, Wake Forest 54-45, and North Carolina State 45-34 for Cameron's third and final Southern Conference title. Duke ended the season 22-2, which still ranks as the fourth-best single-season winning percentage in Duke history.

The NCAA Tournament had started in 1939, and it was comprised of just eight teams, only one from the South. Despite going 22-2 and winning the Southern Conference title, the 1942 Duke team did not receive one of those coveted eight spots. Kentucky took the spot reserved for a Southern school. In fact, despite capturing three Southern Conference titles, Eddie Cameron never coached a postseason game.

Shortly after Pearl Harbor Duke's football coach Wallace Wade joined the United States Army. Cameron took over as head coach of the Duke football team and gave up the basketball team. He ended his hoops career with a 226-99 record. Only Mike Krzyzewski has won more games at Duke.

Chapter 2
BUILDING THE PROGRAM

GERRY GERARD

Eddie Cameron gave up basketball in the early days of World War II. Duke had no desire to initiate a major search under these trying conditions. They literally looked down the hall and found Kenneth Carlyle "Gerry" Gerard—Cameron's assistant coach, a physical education professor, the head soccer coach, and the head of the school's intramural sports program. Schools got lots of mileage out of their coaches in those days. Gerard had been at Duke since 1931 but had been Cameron's assistant for only two seasons. A native of Indiana, Gerard had played football at Illinois as a reserve halfback. He frequently claimed that his primary responsibility was to give water to the starting halfback, the immortal Red Grange.

Gerard was known for his dry wit. On a Duke media questionnaire, he answered the question "favorite cigarette" with "stumps." His "favorite brand of beer" was "plenty." "Do you prefer blondes, brunettes, or redheads?" Gerard answered, "brunette wives and blonde babies."

WORLD WAR II HOOPS

Gerry Gerard's first three seasons as head coach were during World War II. Opponents included such previously unheard of foes as Carolina Preflight, Camp Butner, the Charleston Coast Guard

Station, and the Norfolk Naval Air Station. Players came and went. Some players with military obligations could only play on weekends.

Travel restrictions kept crowds at a bare minimum. An account of one game complains, "There were not more than 100 spectators on hand, in addition to a small band of students. It was a fraternity meeting night and no co-ed night, the feminine students being confined to quarters on Monday nights."

"There definitely is not as much interest in basketball as there was before the war," Eddie Cameron observed in 1944. "The crowds at Duke have amounted to only a handful."

In 1944 Duke ended the regular season 10-13, but eight of the losses were to military bases. The Devils then proceeded to defeat William and Mary, North Carolina State, and North Carolina for the Southern Conference title.

On January 23, 1945, Duke lost to Norfolk Training Station 59-37. Former Blue Devil Bob Gantt led the Sailors with 12 points.

BOB GANTT

In the 1930s and 1940s many of Duke's top basketball players were not hoops specialists. Seasons were shorter, and top athletes commonly played two or even three sports. Bob Gantt was one of the most successful multisport stars. The Durham native starred for Duke's football team as an All-America end in the 1940s. In 1942 *Look* magazine called him "Dixie's Finest Athlete." Gantt spent his autumns on the football field and his springs on the track, where he was a Southern Conference champion in both the discus and the shot put.

Cold weather found Gantt on the basketball court. The six-foot-three 212-pounder was Duke's starting center. He averaged more than 10 points per game as a junior and senior and won Eddie Cameron's praise as "the finest under-the-basket player I have seen in 18 years."

"I never got tired of practicing and training," Gantt claimed. "I always felt my opponents were just as tired as I was. I just had to keep going."

Gantt also is the answer to a trivia question. After serving in the United States Navy during World War II and before beginning a long career as a hospital administrator, Gantt played 23 games for the 1947 Washington Capitals. Duke's first NBA player averaged three points per game for the Caps.

GORDON CARVER

Perhaps no Duke athlete better epitomizes the war years better than Gordon Carver. Like Bob Gantt, Carver was a Durham native who competed in football, basketball, and track. Carver came along just after Gantt and the Loftis brothers. Carver was an outstanding student. He was accepted to Duke on an academic scholarship and planned to be a surgeon so he didn't want to risk his hands by playing sports. He was a hard sell for Wallace Wade and Eddie Cameron, but they persevered and convinced him to continue his sporting career.

They got an exceptional athlete. Carver started out playing baseball in the spring, but Wade convinced him that track was better for his conditioning. Carver ran the 100-yard dash in 9.7 seconds. He was a quarterback who helped Duke lead the nation in scoring in 1943. Carver graduated in three years and entered Duke Medical School as part of the Navy's V-12 program. Thus, he was in medical school and the Navy while playing football and basketball at Duke. Of course, by this time Wade's decision to serve in the military meant that Cameron was now the football coach and Gerry Gerard the basketball coach. North Carolina football coach Carl Snavely so feared Carver's abilities as a defensive back that he told his team, "Don't throw the ball near Gordon, because he is not only a good defensive halfback but a basketball player, a track man, and he can jump higher and run faster than anyone on our team."

The 6-foot-1 Carver was a standout on the hardcourt. He led Duke in scoring in 1944 and was All-Southern Conference in 1944 and 1945. His greatest game came New Year's Day 1944 when he scored 27 points at Madison Square Garden against local favorites Long Island University. Duke led most of the game, but LIU tied it at the buzzer and won 59-57 in overtime. New York writer Sam Davis wrote, "Carver is one of the finest floor men I've seen and in addition is one of the most uncanny shots basketball fans ever have seen in the Garden."

TAKING THE GARDEN

The January 1, 1944, game against Long Island was Duke's first appearance in fabled Madison Square Garden. Although Hall of Fame LIU coach Clair Bee missed the 1944 season because of military service, Long Island was still a high-profile opponent.

Duke didn't have much time for sightseeing. All of the players were in the Navy's V-12 officer's training program and Navy rules limited absences from campus to 48 hours. Duke arrived by train late only a few hours before game time. Duke jumped to a 33-28 halftime lead and extended it to 44-35 with 10 minutes left. Duke tried to milk the clock, but it backfired. Long Island came back and tied the game at 48-48, 50-50, and 51-51. Gene Bledsoe gave Duke a 53-51 lead with 30 seconds left, but LIU tied it at the buzzer. Duke ran out of gas in the overtime and lost 59-57. Gordon Carver ended with 27 points, the most point scored by a college player in the Garden that season. The crowd of more than 16,000 was the largest ever to see the Blue Devils play at the time.

Associated Press' Orlo Robertson wrote, "Carver is one of the best shots we have seen in the Garden all season.

"I think Duke would have done better if they had played the same rushing game in the last 10 minutes of the game as they did in the first 10 minutes."

DUKE'S POW

John Seward attended high school in Newport News, Virginia. His high school played a few games against college freshman teams. In 1940 his team visited Duke, and Seward was so impressive that he was offered a scholarship. He entered Duke along with the Durham High School contingent of Bob Gantt and the Loftis brothers.

Seward made the Southern Conference All-Tournament team in 1943. He then left Duke to serve in the U.S. Army. As a member of the 103rd Infantry, Seward was captured by Germans in 1944. He was a prisoner of war until liberated in April 1945, only weeks before the war's end. He came back to Duke and starred on the 1946 and 1947 teams. Seward averaged about 13 points per game. In 1946 he made the All-Southern Conference Team.

FULL HOUSE

The Duke Indoor Stadium opened in 1940. The Great Depression and World War II combined to keep down attendance. Duke's first home sell-out wasn't until February 28, 1947, when Duke hosted North Carolina. The capacity crowd of 8,800 was touted as the largest crowd to ever see a college basketball game in the South. To the disappointment of most in attendance, Duke fell 57-47 to North Carolina and their euphoniously named center, Nemo Nearman, who scored 14 points. Duke star Ed Koffenberger, playing his final home game, led Duke with 14 points.

NO GAME TONIGHT

Duke was scheduled to play North Carolina State on January 27, 1948, in a key Southern Conference contest. Everett Case was in his second year in Raleigh, and he had turned State into a national power. His high-scoring fast-break offense not only won games, but also excited fans. Too much so on occasion. Reynolds Coliseum was still under construction in 1948, and tiny Thompson Gymnasium couldn't handle the demand. On the day before the game the local newspaper noted, "Less than 50 tickets will be available to the general public with most of the 4,000 seats being occupied by students, wives, dates, and alumni."

Unfortunately, 4,000 people were too many. On the morning of the game North Carolina Insurance commissioner William P. Hodges informed State officials that Thompson Gym could not be used for crowds of more than 1,200. The reason cited was inadequate fire exits. Signs reading "Building Condemned. No Game Tonite" were placed on doors. The game was canceled.

It was rescheduled later in the season at Raleigh's Memorial Auditorium. State won easily 70-37.

GERARD'S ILLNESS

In March 1949 Gerry Gerard became ill and was diagnosed with cancer. He underwent surgery and surprised many observers when he recovered enough to coach Duke in the 1949-1950 season. His declining health forced him to give up coaching shortly before the beginning of the 1950-1951 season. He died January 17, 1951. He was 47 years old. He ended his Duke tenure with a 131-78 record.

RED AUERBACH

When Gerry Gerard became ill, Duke hired a promising 32-year-old coach, Arnold "Red" Auerbach, to be Gerard's assistant. It was assumed that Auerbach would succeed Gerard. However, Auerbach left after a few months.

"Well, [Gerard] lasted a while, but meanwhile I felt pretty bad waiting for him to die," he later wrote. "No way to get a job."

Auerbach went on to win nine NBA championships as head coach of the fabled Boston Celtics. Auerbach did leave one positive benefit for Duke. He made Dick Groat his special project, regularly working with him after practice.

"We played one-on-one every single day in the Indoor Stadium," Groat recalls. "It was like a disease I couldn't cure, loving to play against Red. I couldn't wait to get to practice."

HAROLD BRADLEY

Harold Bradley is the forgotten man in the list of great Duke coaches. Bradley took over under some of the most difficult circumstances imaginable. Yet he quickly won over a team that didn't know him. In his nine years in Durham, Bradley took Duke to its first top 10 appearances and its first NCAA Tournament. Bradley never had a losing season and compiled an ACC winning percentage that places him in the top five in conference history.

Bradley attended tiny Hartwick College. He thought about becoming a physician but couldn't resist the lure of coaching. He coached for a few years in high school before returning to Hartwick. His 50-18 mark there demonstrated ability but hardly set the world on fire. Bradley wrote Eddie Cameron about the Duke position when Gerard had to step down. Cameron was impressed by the letter and heard good things through the grapevine. Bradley took over in November 1950.

Bradley was a quiet, self-effacing man, who emphasized sportsmanship and composure. He lost his temper rarely, and he never cursed. Competing against flamboyant coaches such as North Carolina State's Everett Case and North Carolina's Frank McGuire, it was easy for Bradley to get lost in the crowd.

"Bradley was the consummate gentlemen," Fred Shabel maintains. "His ability to maintain his cool under difficult circumstances was truly impressive."

Tony Drago, Bradley's assistant in the middle 1950s, concurs.

"Bradley was a fierce competitor. He burned inside, but he kept it inside. He was always cool, calm, and collected on the bench. He felt that if he controlled himself, he controlled his team. He was always thinking basketball, 24 hours a day."

LET'S RUN

Howard Bradley wanted to run.

"We had never heard of him," Bernie Janicki says. "We had no idea who he was. He told us he wanted the ball on the glass 100 times a game. We looked at him like he was crazy. But Bradley explained that making one-third of 100 shots was better than making half of 50 shots. After that we loved him.

"The fast-break was our offense. We had a motion offense, but the motion was all vertical—up and down the floor.

"We just ran and ran," teammate Rudy D'Emilio agrees. "We wanted to catch the other team with their pants down."

Before Bradley's arrival, Duke had never scored more than 100 points in a game. They accomplished that feat a dozen times in his tenure. Duke's 1952, 1953, and 1954 teams all finished fourth in the nation in scoring. His 1955 team averaged a school-record 85.2 points per game, a mark that would be impressive in today's game, even though the shot clock and three-point shot were still a generation away.

DICK GROAT

Duke had several basketball All-Americans before the 1950s, but Dick Groat was the school's first consensus All-American. The Pennsylvania native came to Duke to play baseball for Jack Coombs. He was a standout shortstop and led Duke to the 1952 College World Series. He went on to a 14-year major league career, which included winning the 1960 National League Most Valuable Player Award.

But Gerry Gerard and Howard Bradley were delighted to have Groat spend his winters on the basketball court. Barely six feet tall, Groat lacked exceptional quickness, strength, or leaping ability, but his intelligence, skills, and competitiveness made him a standout on the hardcourt.

Groat's father would have preferred that his talented son stick to baseball. Remember that there was a lot more money in professional baseball than professional basketball in the 1950s. Like many people who have attended Duke, a campus visit was the key.

Dick Groat against Temple in 1951. *Mark Kauffman/Time Life Pictures/Getty Images*

"I remember how impressed I was with the Indoor Stadium," Groat recalls. "At that time it was the finest basketball facility in the South. I'd never seen a field house like Duke's at that time. I was fascinated by it."

Several of Groat's individual efforts stand out. On January 6, 1951, hoops fans eagerly awaited the matchup between Groat and North Carolina State's Sammy Ranzino, each of whom was ranked among the nation's top 10 scorers. Groat won the individual duel 36 to 32, but State won the game 77-71 in overtime. Duke led 67-59 with six minutes left but could not score the rest of regulation. Helping temporarily shut down Groat was State defensive stopper Vic Bubas, the future Duke coach. Groat's 36 points established a school single-game scoring record. It lasted only three weeks. On January 29 Groat set a school record with 37 points in a 90-68 win over Davidson. Groat went 17-17 from the foul line in that game. Groat ended the season averaging 25.2 points per game, fourth in the nation. He was named National Player of the Year by UPI and by the Helms Athletic Foundation.

If anything Groat was even better in 1952. He averaged 26 points per game, still the second-best mark in Duke history. In his final home game, on February 29, 1952, Groat scored a stunning 48 points to lead Duke to a 94-64 rout over North Carolina. He hit 19 field goals and 10 free throws and threw in a dozen assists for good measure. Duke ended both the 1951 and 1952 seasons by losing to Everett Case's Wolfpack in the Southern Conference Tournament finals. Duke finished the 1952 season ranked 12th the AP poll, the first time Duke had ever ended a season nationally ranked. Groat was on all of the All-America teams and repeated as Southern Conference Player of the Year. His 26 points and 7.6 assists per game were both second in the nation. Later that spring Groat led the Duke baseball team to the College World Series. On May 1, 1952, Duke retired his number 12. He was the first Duke athlete to have his number retired.

REBOUND

Dick Groat's 48 points wasn't the only school record set on that night against North Carolina. Duke's Bernie Janicki pulled down 31 rebounds, which still is a school record. Only 6-foot-3, Janicki seemed an unlikely candidate to be a dominating rebounder. But dominating he was.

JANICKI'S SECRET?

"It was just desire," he explains. "I thought every rebound was mine. If no one was in the way, I went for the ball. If someone was in the way, I went around them or through them."

Janicki averaged 15.9 rebounds per game in 1959, the best single-season average in Duke history. He averaged 11.1 for his Duke career.

THEY REALLY LIKE HIM

Fred Shabel was a sophomore reserve in 1952. His parents came down to Durham from New Jersey at the end of the 1952 season to see their first college basketball game. This was the game against North Carolina when Dick Groat scored 48 points. Coach Howard Bradley took Groat out with seconds left and replaced him with Shabel. Naturally, Groat received a prolonged standing ovation.

After the game Shabel's parents were beaming.

"Freddie, did you see how much they like you?" they told their son. "Everybody stood and cheered when you went into the game."

Shabel never did tell his parents that the cheers were for Groat, not him.

THE DIXIE CLASSIC

The Dixie Classic was a holiday tournament held every year from 1949 to 1960. North Carolina State's Reynolds Coliseum hosted the three-day affair during the week between Christmas and New Year's. North Carolina State, North Carolina, Duke, and Wake Forest competed annually but were joined by four outside schools. Each team played three times. These visitors weren't the cupcakes so often found in holiday classics; rather they were potent national powers such as West Virginia, Villanova, Michigan State, or DePaul. In 1958 the legendary Oscar Robertson brought his top-ranked Cincinnati team to Raleigh and left with a pair of losses.

Vic Bubas played in the very first Dixie Classic and coached in the event as an assistant at North Carolina State and head coach at Duke.

"It was a fun time of the year," Bubas remembers. "We wanted to win the Dixie Classic, but we didn't have the pressure that we had in the conference tournament when only the winner advanced. The tournament could not have been successful without the involvement of all of the local teams. It eventually became in my opinion the finest holiday tournament in the country. So many things going on made it a festive, fair atmosphere."

THE GREAT COMEBACK

In 1950 Duke lost its Dixie Classic opener to Colgate 84-69. They regrouped for a 71-63 win over UNC. This matched them against Tulane for fifth place. It looked like a losing proposition when Tulane jumped to a 54-22 lead late in the first half. Duke went into the locker room trailing 56-27. At one point Tulane had outscored Duke 30-2. During one timeout referee Arnold Heff quipped, "I better change basketballs. This one is so hot I can't handle it."

Duke still trailed 72-52 with about eight minutes left. Then Dick Groat went to work. The junior guard was unstoppable. He scored 24 points after intermission. With the score 72-58, Groat scored 10 unanswered points. One account called him "a wizard with the basketball, hitting from all angles and driving through the weary Tulane defense for basket after basket." Tulane went ice cold from the field. When they tried to hold the ball, they turned it over.

Groat tied the score 72-72 with a minute left. Duke forced another turnover, and Dayton Allen gave Duke a two-point lead. Tulane couldn't score, and Duke held on for a 74-72 win. Duke had outscored Tulane 47-16 in the second half, 22-0 down the stretch. Groat ended the game with 32 points. The comeback from a 32-point deficit remains the largest in NCAA history.

"[This game] proves we are all crazy for ever getting into this business," North Carolina coach Tom Rogers told a companion after witnessing the game. "It gives you ulcers or heart trouble—or both."

Duke coach Howard Bradley was more succinct.

"I never saw anything like it."

WINNING THE TITLE

Duke had moderate success in the Dixie Classic. The Devils always won at least one of their three games. In 1953 Duke captured its only Dixie Classic championship. It was an unexpected title. Duke wasn't expected to get past its opener against 12th-ranked Oregon State. The

Beavers featured a huge front line that included 7-foot-2 Swede Halbrook. Duke's strategy was simple. Run their bigger foes to death.

"Coach Bradley said we would wear them out, and we did," Bernie Janicki remembers. "By the end of the game they were exhausted."

Duke won 71-61 and went on to defeat Wake Forest 83-66 and Navy 98-83 for the title. Guard Rudy D'Emilio scored 66 points in the three games and won MVP honors.

THE ACC

In May 1953 seven Southern Conference schools met in Greensboro and decided to form a new conference. Duke was one of these schools, along with longtime rivals North Carolina, North Carolina State, Wake Forest, Clemson, South Carolina, and Maryland. Virginia joined later in the year. After considering such names as the Dixie League, the Tobacco League, and the Piedmont League, the circuit was named the Atlantic Coast Conference. It eventually became known as the nation's top collegiate basketball conference. Fittingly, Duke's first Atlantic Coast Conference game was a victory, 86-64 over Virginia. In the ACC's first 52 seasons, Duke would lose more conference games than it won only nine times.

Duke's first ACC team won the Dixie Classic and entered the Associated Press top 10 for the first time in school history. Duke defeated nemesis North Carolina State twice in the regular season 87-85 and 90-89. In the second game Duke trailed State 87-82 at Reynolds Coliseum with 2:30 left but rode several key steals to a comeback win. Duke finished the regular season with a 9-1 conference mark.

THE TOURNAMENT

The ACC had continued an old Southern Conference tradition. The league champion and the ACC's bid to the NCAA Tournament would be decided in a conference tournament. Duke's first-place finish in 1954 entitled them to a high seed and nothing else. Even worse, the tournament would be held on the North Carolina State campus at Reynolds Coliseum. This made sense, at least financial sense. With a capacity of 12,400 Reynolds was by far the largest arena in the area. But it placed the other seven schools at a competitive disadvantage.

"We didn't think it was fair," Janicki recalls, "but it was the largest place around, and money talks."

Of course, Duke had hosted the Southern Conference Tournament four times and never came away with a championship.

Duke was seeded No. 1. The Devils handily defeated Virginia in the opener, which placed them against fourth-seeded North Carolina State in the semifinals. Duke played a tough game against State but couldn't pull off a third win against Everett Case's Wolfpack, falling 79-75. The home team outshot Duke 50-25 from the foul line.

State went on to defeat Wake Forest for the first ACC championship. Duke was invited to the NIT but declined.

"This was just after the point-shaving scandals in New York," Bernie Janicki explains, "and they were afraid we would be corrupted by playing in New York. It was a big disappointment."

TEAM OF COACHES

The 1954 team could be called the team of coaches. One of the reserves was senior forward Charles Driesell, already known by his nickname "Lefty." Driesell, of course, went on to torment Duke for years as coach at Davidson and then Maryland. Driesell averaged a modest five points per game in 1954, but that was still more than fellow reserve Fred Shabel, also a senior that year. Shabel would be an assistant at Duke under Vic Bubas before moving to Connecticut, where he coached the Huskies to the 1964 Eastern Regional Finals, where they lost to Duke.

Although Driesell and Shabel were reserves, the same can't be said about sophomore guard Joe Belmont, who scored more than 12 points per game for the 1954 Blue Devils. Belmont went on to become the 1970 ABA Coach of the Year with the Denver Nuggets.

A REAL CUTIE

Joe Belmont was perhaps the flashiest player in Duke history. The 5-foot-11 guard came along during a time when Boston Celtics great Bob Cousy had made behind-the-back dribbling and passing both popular and effective. Belmont was almost Cousy's equal.

"Joe could do anything Cousy could do," teammate Bernie Janicki asserts. "If he had been on TV as much as today's players, he would have been a legend."

Belmont came from Philadelphia, where he teamed with future Temple and NBA star Guy Rodgers at Northeast Public High School. Belmont was a crowd-pleaser, but he also was a tough, savvy competitor.

"[Belmont] was a cutie out there," longtime ACC referee Lou Bello said. "He'd beat you somehow. He'd tug at your shirt, push you on a layup. He knew how to get away with things, but boy could he play."

Belmont averaged 13 points per game and was named first-team All-ACC in 1956. He turned down a chance to play in the NBA, preferring the stability of a regular job and the trucking business, alongside a playing career with the Denver-Chicago Truckers of the National Industrial Basketball League. He eventually became a professional referee and coach.

THE BIG DANCE

In recent years Duke has been a regular participant in the NCAA Tournament, but this wasn't always the case. The tournament was first held in 1939 and was made up of only eight teams. The tournament gradually expanded but despite some outstanding teams, Duke always fell short, frequently to Everett Case's powerhouse teams from North Carolina State. In 1955, however, State was on probation because of recruiting irregularities. In those days the winner of the ACC Tournament received the conference's only spot in the NCAAs. An easy win over South Carolina and an overtime triumph over Virginia sent Duke into the ACC Tournament finals against none other than State. Even though State defeated Duke 87-77 to win the championship, the runner-up Devils received their first invitation to the NCAAs.

Reaction on campus was subdued.

"The team was excited about playing in the NCAA, and our friends were happy on our account," Duke player Junior Morgan remembers. "But there were no banners or pep rallies or anything. It was pretty matter of fact."

Duke's first game was at New York's fabled Madison Square Garden, against Villanova. The game was part of a tripleheader. In a time when college basketball rarely was televised, Duke knew nothing about the Wildcats.

"I believe we can beat Villanova although I haven't seen the team play," Duke coach Harold Bradley told the media. "It's tough to prepare for a team you've never seen play."

No amount of preparation helps a team that shoots 9-35 in the first half, as was the case with Duke. Still, trailing 39-29 at the intermission, Duke hung tough. When star forward Ronnie Mayer fouled out with four minutes left, Duke trailed 69-57, and their season appeared to be over. The resilient Devils forced some turnovers and fought their way back into the game. Duke trailed 74-71 with 10 seconds left when Bob Lakata was fouled. Lakata planned to make the first free throw and miss the second deliberately. He missed both, but Morgan rebounded the second and scored, making the score 74-73. Villanova inbounded the ball and played keep-away until the final buzzer.

Bradley felt that his team suffered from stage fright.

"I'm afraid our boys were too awestruck over appearing in Madison Square Garden."

Not of all his players agreed.

"After three games in three days in the ACC Tournament we were tired," Mayer recalled. "Nothing worked. We weren't ready. We weren't intimidated by Madison Square Garden. In fact, we were disappointed. The Garden wasn't a special place. I thought it was a pit. After playing for the ACC title in front of 12,000 rabid State fans in Reynolds Coliseum, we weren't scared of Madison Square Garden."

"Madison Square Garden was a hostile atmosphere, but we were not unaccustomed to playing in a hostile atmosphere," Morgan adds. "It's not like we were a bunch of country bumpkins walking down the streets of the big city wondering how the buildings got so tall."

AUTOGRAPH PLEASE

Freshmen weren't eligible most of this period. Freshman teams played other freshman teams but also sometimes played military teams. In 1955 one of these military teams came to Duke to play the frosh. The visitors included Richie Regan, a recent All-American at Seton Hall. Freshman coach Tony Drago was going over defensive assignments before the game. He assigned Bobby Joe Harris the task of guarding Regan.

"I don't want to guard Regan," the awestruck teenager informed Drago, "I want to ask him for his autograph."

PLEASE DON'T HURT ME

In February 1956 Duke visited Lexington to play the eighth-ranked Kentucky Wildcats. Duke trailed much of the way but made a late rally. It fell short, and Kentucky won 81-76. Sophomore reserve Hayes Clement watched most of the game from the bench. As he was walking to the locker room after the end of the game, something amazing happened.

"I was attacked by a little old lady, probably about 75 years old. She started hitting me with her umbrella, while screaming, 'You almost beat us! You almost beat us.' I yelled, 'Don't take it out on me! I didn't have anything to do with it.' Imagine what would have happened if we had won."

THE CATS GO DOWN

There's little question that Kentucky was the nation's most recognizable college basketball program in the 1950s. On December 18, 1956, the seventh-ranked Wildcats visited Duke Indoor Stadium for the first time to take on the 13th-ranked Blue Devils. Duke had visited Kentucky the previous season and had played the Wildcats before losing 81-76. Much of that Duke team had graduated.

"Kentucky was one of the top programs in the country," Duke's Bucky Allen remembers, "but we were playing at home, and we were always confident when we were playing at home. Most of us hadn't played the year before against Kentucky, so we wanted our shot."

Kentucky jumped to a 30-15 lead midway through the first half and still led 53-40 early in the second half. However, Kentucky playmaker Gerry Calvert fouled out with 14 minutes left. Duke went to a full-court press and began eating into the lead.

"It was almost like coach [Howard] Bradley knew what was going to happen," Allen says. "We had given extra attention to the press in practices leading up to the game. He must have been psychic."

It paid off in a big way. Bobby Joe Harris, a quick 5-foot-10 guard, forced numerous turnovers. Harris had three steals in the final two minutes. The last came with Duke trailing 84-83 with less than 30 seconds remaining. Harris passed the ball to Allen for the layup and an 85-84 lead. Incredibly, it was Duke's first lead of the game. Kentucky missed a free throw with seconds left, and Duke escaped with the win.

"Harris won the game," Allen maintains. "I got all the publicity, but he won the game."

Duke scored the last 10 points of the contest. It was Duke's first victory over Kentucky since the 1930 Southern Conference Tournament and the only time Duke has defeated the Wildcats in Durham.

NOT A HAPPY CAMPER

During the 1950s, the Duke locker room and the visitor's locker room were not far apart, and after beating Kentucky, the players were able to listen to the Wildcats' reaction.

"We heard lots of cussing from the Kentucky locker room," Hayes Clement remembers. "Loud cussing. Then loud noises. Stuff being thrown, tables being overturned. [Coach Adolph] Rupp wasn't happy, and he didn't care who knew it."

Bobby Joe Harris made the mistake of going into the Kentucky locker room to speak to Vern Hatton, an old friend.

"I shouldn't have done that," Harris recalls. "Rupp jumped in my face and told me emphatically and colorfully that I had no business being there. He didn't have to tell me twice."

KEEPING TRACK

Harold Bradley would carry a stack of three-by-five notecards to every practice and every game. When a player made a mistake, he would jot something down on a notecard and wait for the right time to elaborate on the mistake.

"We would joke about the notecards all the time," Bobby Joe Harris remembers. "Make a mistake and get carded. He never wrote down the good stuff, just the bad. We would look over and see Coach Bradley writing, and we knew we were going to get it during the next timeout."

RAIDING PENNSYLVANIA

Beginning with Dick Groat, Duke had tremendous success recruiting players from Pennsylvania. Bernie Janicki, Joe Belmont, Ronnie Mayer, Rudy D'Emilio, Paul Schmidt, and Doug Kistler were among the other top players recruited from that state by Howard

Bradley. The 1954 Duke team featured no less than six players from Pennsylvania. Vic Bubas continued that trend with Jack Marin, Steve Vacendak, Bob Riedy, and Dick DeVenzio, among others. Every Duke team in the ACC had at least one player from Pennsylvania until the 1968 team.

Much of Duke's success in Pennsylvania came from Groat's popularity.

"We weren't all sure where Duke was, but we knew who Dick Groat was," Janicki recalls. "We figured that if Duke was good enough for Groat, it was good enough for us."

"We had a good pipeline in Pennsylvania in part because of the large number of Duke alumni in the area," freshman coach Tony Drago adds. "We didn't have huge recruiting budgets in those days. It was like drilling for oil. If you found a good spot, you kept going back."

HOSTING THE CHAMPS

On six occasions Duke has hosted a team that would go on to win the NCAA title. The first time this happened was March 1, 1957, when Frank McGuire brought his University of North Carolina Tar Heels over to Durham before an overflow crowd estimated at 9,000. UNC was 24-0 and ranked No. 1 in the country. They played to that level in the first half, especially All-America forward Lennie Rosenbluth. Duke tried almost everyone on Rosenbluth, but he still scorched Duke for 24 first-half points. Not surprisingly Duke trailed 47-35.

Howard Bradley's team fought back after intermission and took a 70-69 lead with less than four minutes to play. With their undefeated season on the line, UNC pulled away down the stretch, winning 86-72. Rosenbluth finished with 40 points, while Bobby Joe Harris and Paul Schmidt led Duke with 19 and 16 points respectively.

The game was controversial. Duke was called for a staggering 35 fouls and had five players disqualified. UNC made 36 of 54 free throws. The angry crowd littered the floor with debris, mostly paper megaphones, while McGuire claimed to have been pelted with an apple. North Carolina went on to finish 32-0 and defeat Kansas to win the NCAA title. Hayes Clement feels that the officials were protecting Rosenbluth.

"He was a great scorer, no question. But if you looked at him the wrong way, the refs would send him to the foul line."

WOOLEN GYM

The University of North Carolina played its home games in the 1950s at Woolen Gymnasium, a modest facility that barely could seat 5,000. Bucky Allen remembers this was something of a problem.

"Fans would scream insults and throw stuff at us throughout the game. During timeouts we had to bring chairs out to the middle of court. It got so bad that [coach Howard] Bradley found about 15 of the biggest and meanest Duke football players he could find and took them over to the games. They would sit behind the Duke bench and give us some protection."

WATCHING THE CLOCK

Duke and North Carolina had some controversial games in the 1950s. None was more unusual than the 1957 matchup in Chapel Hill. Duke trailed the undefeated Tar Heels most of the game until a Bobby Joe Harris field goal tied the game 73-73 with only a few seconds left. However, the ancient hand-operated scoreboard didn't immediately record the last Duke basket. Harris looked at the scoreboard and saw that Duke was trailing by two. He fouled UNC's Tommy Kearns in order to stop the clock. After Kearns was headed to the foul line, Harris looked again and saw the adjusted score.

"What have I done?" Harris muttered.

Kearns sank the shots, and Duke lost 75-73.

"It still bothers me," Harris says. "What a terrible way to lose a game."

PAYBACK TIME

Duke went back to Chapel Hill in 1958 determined to make up for the disappointing loss the season before. Playing an almost perfect game, Duke upset the defending national champions 91-75. Harris called timeout with only a few seconds left and the game well in hand. An incredulous coach Howard Bradley demanded to know what he doing.

"Well, Coach," replied Harris. "I just wanted to give them time to get the score right. They've rubbed our noses in it long enough."

Bradley nodded and responded quietly, "Maybe you're right."

The team sat down on the bench and waited out the timeout without Bradley saying another word.

WHY ARE THEY CHEERING?

In January 1958 Duke went up north to play New York University in Madison Square Garden. Duke was a slight favorite and led most of the way on the way to a 67-60 win.

"[The crowd was] not very loud for most of the game," Hayes Clement recalls. "Some noise but less than we would hear in an ACC game. Then with about five minutes left they started roaring after every basket. The game was close, but it wasn't that close. The lead wasn't changing hands, but they were screaming after every field goal. I didn't understand it at the time. After the game, somebody informed me that most of the fans had money bet on the point spread. It wasn't the score that was important, it was the margin. I guess I was a naïve country boy, but it was the first I had heard about that stuff. It was a real eye-opener."

McGUIRE AND MURRAY

In 1958 North Carolina visited Duke for the regular-season finale. The teams were tied atop the ACC standings with 10-3 records. Tempers flared late in the game when Paul Schmidt and UNC's Lee Shaffer got into a brief scuffle going for a rebound. Officials conferred with Howard Bradley and Frank McGuire and warned both teams.

Duke won the game 59-46. Giddy Duke students rushed the floor at the game's conclusion and cut down the nets. McGuire kept his UNC team on the bench for a conspicuous 15 minutes before they went to their locker room.

Duke football coach Bill Murray was acting athletic director, because Eddie Cameron was out of town. Murray was furious with McGuire.

"It was an uncalled-for demonstration. In all my coaching experience, I have never seen a more obnoxious demonstration. It is the most revolting display by a coach I have ever witnessed. The very idea of McGuire demanding police protection to be escorted to his dressing room is absurd. He has created a monster in his publicity-seeking statements."

"I wish Murray had come to me with those remarks," McGuire shot back. "I'd tell him he had enough to worry about in [UNC coach] Jim Tatum to keep him occupied."

They continued to squabble in the press for weeks.

Bucky Allen recalls coming out of the locker room after showering and dressing.

"I couldn't believe the UNC team was still at their bench. There couldn't have been more than 100 Duke students still there. Everybody else had left. I asked a UNC player what was going on and was told, 'Coach McGuire is pulling another one of his stunts.'"

NO. 1 GOES DOWN

Duke has defeated the No. 1 team in the country eight times. The first time this happened was January 27, 1958. The victims were the West Virginia Mountaineers, who came to Durham sporting a fancy 14-0 mark and fully expecting to go 15-0. West Virginia had a huge size advantage on the Devils. Duke's tallest starters were a pair of 6-foot-5 players, Paul Schmidt and Jim Newcombe, while West Virginia was led by 6-foot-10 All-American Lloyd Sharrar. What Duke lacked in size, however, they more than made up for in experience. All five of Duke's starters were seniors.

Duke combated West Virginia's size with a stifling zone defense that held Sharrar to nine points and none after intermission. Meanwhile the quicker Devils found openings in the West Virginia defense.

Bobby Joe Harris had the unenviable task of guarding West Virginia's sophomore sensation, Jerry West.

"He was too much for me. When I played off him, he would shoot and score. When I played him tight, he would drive by me and score. During a timeout [coach Howard] Bradley yelled at me, 'What's the matter? Can't you guard this guy?' I screamed back, 'No, I can't. Why don't you try it?'"

Bucky Allen had no more success.

"I couldn't handle him. He was the best I ever played against, by far."

Despite West's heroics, Duke held off the Mountaineers 72-68. After the loss, West Virginia coach Fred Schaus quipped, "Maybe this

Carolina air isn't too good for our boys. Someday I hope we can come down and show you we've got a ball club."

ON THE BENCH?

One day in 1958 coach Howard Bradley ended a practice by instructing his players to go to the spot on the floor where they expected to take the majority of their shots in the next game. Bobby Joe Harris and Bucky Allen went to the wings. Jim Newcombe and Paul Schmidt went to the lane. Reserve center Larry Bateman went to the bench and started taking 50-foot hook shots at the goal. The incredulous Bradley asked him what he was doing.

"Well, you told us to practice shooting from where we thought we would be in the next game," Bateman responded. "I expect to be here, on the bench."

THE CHINESE FACTOR

In late 1958 Duke went to Virginia, taking an 11-game winning streak with them. Virginia wasn't very good in those days, but Duke had several players injured or ill. Virginia upset Duke 70-68 in triple overtime.

"It was pretty bad in the locker room," Hayes Clement recalls. "Lots of cussing, lots of moaning, lots of groaning. [Coach Howard] Bradley wasn't saying much. He seemed really down. Bob Lakata turned to Bradley and said, 'Cheer up, Coach. There are a billion Chinese who don't even know we played tonight.'"

DEATH VALLEY

The ACC was a geographically compact league in the 1950s, but that didn't mean road trips were easy. Hayes Clement recalls trips to Clemson.

"First we took the bus, so we were exhausted when we got there. Clemson played in a bandbox, not much bigger than a high school gym. They would fill it up. Add a band of 100 playing 'Hold That Tiger' or 'Tiger Rag' every chance they got, and it was so loud you couldn't hear yourself think. Coach [Howard] Bradley would have us take chairs onto the center of the court during timeouts. It was the only way you could hear yourself think."

But it wasn't just the noise, says Clement.

"The Clemson football team would sit right behind the Duke bench and spend the entire game peppering us with rubber bands, spitballs, and insults. If you were running down the court near the sidelines, you could expect someone to stick out a leg and try to trip you."

Still, Clemson only beat Duke once in the 1950s, a 56-55 win in December 1958. But Duke was always glad to get on the bus back to Durham.

BRADLEY LEAVES

Successful ACC basketball coaches rarely walk away from their jobs at the peak of their careers. In the spring of 1959 Harold Bradley dropped a bombshell, when he announced that he was leaving Duke for the same position at the University of Texas. This was more an attraction to Texas than any dissatisfaction with Duke. Texas had more financial resources than Duke. They offered Bradley $12,000 per year and agreed to give him more scholarships to work with than had been the case at Duke. The Southwestern Conference was a football league, and Bradley didn't have to contend with giant shadows of Everett Case and Frank McGuire. The Texas program was struggling, and Bradley was intrigued by the challenge of building a team.

"Dad loved Duke, but he just felt like Texas was an opportunity he couldn't turn down," Bradley's son Bob recalls.

Bradley left Duke with a 167-78 record. He had considerable success at Texas, taking the Longhorns to two NCAA Tournaments in eight seasons, before retiring.

Chapter 3

THE BUBAS YEARS

FINDING A NEW COACH

Harold Bradley left the Duke program in pretty good shape. Under him Duke had achieved success in a top conference and had won its share of high-profile non-conference games. Duke had a top-notch facility and high name recognition. Not surprisingly, interest in the job was high. Duke athletic director Eddie Cameron sifted through some 135 applications and interviewed 10 finalists. In the end the job went to a candidate who hadn't even been interviewed. Cameron went a mere 25 miles down U.S. Highway 70 to hire North Carolina State assistant Vic Bubas.

Bubas recently had applied for a vacant Ohio State job, which had gone to Fred Taylor. Bubas turned down a chance to become head coach at Clemson and then applied for the New Mexico job, but they decided to promote from within. Thirty-two years old, Bubas was frustrated and considering leaving coaching when Cameron came calling. The two men met at a local restaurant, shook hands, and that was it. Bubas actually took a slight pay cut in base salary, but Cameron agreed to let Bubas make extra money in the summer. Bubas quickly turned the Duke Basketball Camp into a top summer camp for aspiring players.

"I thought it took an awful lot of courage," he recalls. "Eddie gave me my break."

Cameron introduced Bubas at a May 6, 1959, press conference.

Eddie Cameron, Vic Bubas, and vice president Charles Jordan at the press conference announcing Bubas' hiring.

"Gentlemen, this is Vic Bubas, our new basketball coach. We hope he is our coach forever."

BORN TO COACH

Vic Bubas was one of the so-called "Hoosier Hotshots" who came from Everett Case's native Indiana to turn North Carolina State into a national hoops power. The first time Bubas ever met Case, he told him that he wanted to be a head coach someday and wanted to be coached with that in mind. Case was more than willing.

"Enter State, achieve good grades, act as a gentleman at all times, and fight hard on the court," he told Bubas. "If you do that, I will fight just as hard to land a coaching job."

Bubas' father was an immigrant who had started a prosperous hardware store in Gary, Indiana, and wanted his son to stay home and take over the business. When he was finally convinced that was not going to happen, he talked to Case.

"Okay, Victor wants to be coach—you make a damn good coach outta him," he said.

Bubas wasn't a great athlete, wasn't very big, and only averaged about seven points a game. Yet his defense, ball-handling, and overall court intelligence made him a key component in North Carolina State teams that captured four consecutive Southern Conference titles. He was intelligent, analytical, methodical, and well prepared.

"[Bubas] came, he saw, he liked, he stayed," Case quipped.

Bubas remained at State as freshman coach and then moved up to varsity, where he was Case's top assistant. He and Case were so close that State's players called them "Pete and Repeat."

THE FIRST BASKET

Vic Bubas' determination can be seen in an incident from the opening game at Reynolds Coliseum in 1949. Bubas desperately wanted to score the first points in the new building.

"I made up my mind that if I got the opening tap, I was not going to pass," Bubas explains. "I wanted that basket."

He got the opening tap and drove for the basket. He missed a shot, rebounded, missed again, knocked down a teammate to get it again, and finally scored. A few minutes later Case substituted for Bubas and called him over to the bench. Bubas expected to be chewed out, but Case simply smiled.

"You sure wanted that first basket," he said.

THE RIVALRY CONTINUES

After Duke hired Vic Bubas, Everett Case sent Duke a telegram.

"Duke has secured an extremely intelligent young man of the highest caliber to directs its program," it said.

Both men were uncomfortable when their teams met but coached their teams to the hilt. Case beat Bubas four of the first six times they played, but Bubas captured the last six meetings.

"I hated coaching against Case," Bubas says. "It was awkward, but we both had to be adults about it. Once the game tipped off, we forgot everything except winning."

THAT'S AN ORDER

Bubas inherited one assistant coach, Fred Shabel, who had played for Duke in the early 1950s.

"Fred's a Duke guy, and we're going to look out for Duke guys," Eddie Cameron told Vic Bubas. "You have to keep him for one season. If it works out, then he can stay on. If it doesn't, you can make a change. But he gets one year."

It worked out. Shabel was Bubas' top assistant through the 1963 season, when Bubas helped him get the head job at the University of Connecticut.

RECRUITING

After that introductory press conference, Eddie Cameron told Vic Bubas it was time to start recruiting. No one ever responded better to a boss' suggestion. In the 1940s and 1950s, college basketball recruiting tended to be regional. Frank McGuire's "Underground Railroad" funneled prospects from his native New York south to Chapel Hill. Everett Case's North Carolina State program was populated with his "Hoosier Hotshots" from Indiana. Adolph Rupp ruled Kentucky. Recommendations, contacts, and networking were the names of the game. It was not unheard of for coaches to take players sight unseen, relying on a recommendation from a trusted associate. Bubas helped change that.

Duke had been successful in North Carolina and Pennsylvania but rarely recruited away from the East Coast. Bubas expanded Duke's territory. He and his tireless staff would gather information on players when they were juniors and unheard of at the time. Bubas would send newspaper clippings of Duke games to prospects.

Bubas refused to concede any recruit. He stole Art Heyman from under McGuire's nose, brought in Jeff Mullins from Lexington, Kentucky, and filled Duke's roster with talent from as far away as Texas, Illinois, and Indiana. He even brought in All-American Mike Lewis from the unlikely locale of Missoula, Montana. UCLA coach John Wooden once admitted that the Bruins tried to recruit Lewis.

"Every time we called his house, Bucky Waters answered the phone," he confessed.

Waters was a Duke assistant.

"[Bubas] approached coaching as if Duke was a national brand, and he and his coaches were sales managers," Fred Shabel says. "We had to get on the road and sell our product."

"Vic taught us how to recruit," North Carolina coaching great Dean Smith said. "We had been starting on prospects in the fall of their senior year, like almost everybody. But Vic was working on them their junior year. For a while, all of us were trying to catch up with him."

RECRUITING ON THE MOON

Duke player Jay Buckley was an exceptional student in the sciences. He once had a summer internship with NASA. When his interest in NASA was publicized, he was asked if he hoped to be the first person on the moon.

"I would probably find Coach [Vic] Bubas already there, looking for recruits," Buckley replied.

CEO

Vic Bubas was not just a basketball coach. He was the CEO of a corporation. Even though he had taken a pay cut when he took the Duke job, he insisted that Duke upgrade the basketball offices. He expected his assistants to dress like businessmen. He was impressed by UCLA's pep band at the 1962 Final Four. The following season Duke had a pep band. Duke was the first team to put the names of players on the back of their jerseys. Bubas went to dorms, businesses, and civic clubs to promote Duke basketball.

"[Coach Bubas was] the first corporate coach, organized, detailed, and meticulous," Art Heyman explains.

But Bubas isn't completely convinced.

"I'm not sure about all that CEO stuff. I'm not good at self-evaluation. I just tried to go about doing things the right way."

ASSISTANT COACHES

Like all good CEOs, Vic Bubas wasn't afraid to delegate. He wanted assistant coaches whose desire to become head coaches matched the desire he had had at North Carolina State. Bubas had five assistant coaches in his 10 years at Duke. Chuck Daly left after the 1969 season to become head coach at Boston College. He later won a pair of NBA titles as head coach of the Detroit Pistons. Fred Shabel left to become head coach at Connecticut. Likewise Tom Carmody at Rhode Island. Bucky Waters left Duke for West Virginia and would return to Duke to replace Bubas. Hubie Brown went to the NBA, where he coached Kentucky to the 1975 ABA title and was named 1978 and 2004 NBA Coach of the Year. Five assistants, five successful head coaches.

All except for Shabel were hired from the high school ranks.

"I think high school coaches are the best teachers," Bubas says. "They can't recruit. They have to go with whoever shows up, so they have to be adaptable and they have to be able to communicate. That's what I was after."

Like all good bosses, Bubas knew how to delegate.

"If a head coach does all of the talking, players get tired of hearing him. Using your assistants is healthy for everybody. The assistants learn; the players learn. If you are successful, your assistants rightfully have a sense of pride in what you've accomplished."

Waters concurs.

"Vic gave responsibility and accountability to his assistants. He would tell us to ask if we needed help, but if we didn't ask, we were on our own. He would tell us to scout a team and tell us how to beat it, design a play and teach it. You always felt empowered. It was a great learning experience."

POISE AND PRIDE

Vic Bubas wanted his teams to play with poise and pride. In the mid-1960s he explained his philosophy.

"We don't go in too much for blatant emotionalism. It would be impossible to get the players up for each game with a highly emotional tirade such as towel-throwing or sobbing. It would be an insult to their intelligence, and believe me, these are intelligent boys. Pride is the element that makes them champions. They understand what Duke basketball has been for years, and they know what is expected of them. From there, they can figure it out themselves. It's pride that pays off in terms of spirit and hustle in games and in practice."

Jeff Mullins agrees.

"We were always well prepared. Bubas had the rare ability to have us thoroughly prepared without limiting our ability to be creative. We always took the court expecting to win. We wanted to play up to his and our expectations."

WINNER TAKE ALL

From 1954 to 1974 the winner of the Atlantic Coast Conference Tournament was the official conference champion and received the conference's only bid to the NCAA Tournament. A successful regular season established only a high seed for the tournament, a three-day, winner-take-all shootout.

Duke athletic director (and former coach) Eddie Cameron was a big supporter of the tournament and argued against anybody who wanted to eliminate it.

"I think tournament basketball is what brought the ACC out of mediocrity and to the level of excellence we now enjoy," Cameron contends. "That's the reason teams improve. If we lose the tournament, we'll return to mediocre basketball."

Vic Bubas was the most successful ACC Tournament coach in Duke history.

"Today's coaches have no inkling of what real tournament pressure was," Bubas says. "They may think they do, but they don't. You have to live through it."

Bubas learned from the master. He played and coached at North Carolina State under Everett Case, who loved the Southern Conference and ACC tournaments. As a player Bubas was undefeated in four Southern Conference Tournaments.

Case transmitted his enthusiasm for tournaments to Bubas.

"Coach Case thought that tournament basketball was the way to go," Bubas explains. "It promoted the game and gave everyone a chance."

How did Case approach the tournament?

"Other coaches wanted to make things complicated," Bubas remembers. "Case always wanted to simplify things prior to the tournament. About two weeks before the tournament, he would reduce the offense by about one-third and concentrate on fundamentals. His motto was 'Be a different human being. Cut out distractions, reach a physical and mental peak. A lean horse for the long race.'"

The apprentice learned his lessons well. Bubas went 22-6 in 10 ACC Tournaments. He won four, finished second four times, and lost in the second round twice. He is the only Duke coach since the founding of the ACC to never lose in the first round of the tournament.

NOT BAD FOR A ROOKIE

It didn't take Vic Bubas long to demonstrate his tournament abilities. His first Duke team in 1960 didn't have a single senior in the rotation. Bubas experimented with his lineup throughout the season. Duke struggled through a 7-7 ACC regular season and entered the ACC Tournament with a 12-10 overall mark. Yet Bubas employed the tricks he had learned from Case and pulled out an unlikely ACC Tournament title, Duke's first.

After a first-round win over South Carolina, Duke squared off in the semifinals against a powerful North Carolina squad ranked 16th. The Tar Heels already had defeated Duke three times (once in the Dixie Classic) by margins of 22, 26, and 25 points. Bubas went to a 1-3-1 zone that held UNC scoreless for six minutes. Duke jumped to a 35-23 halftime lead and withstood a furious UNC rally to hold on for a 71-69 win. Carroll Youngkin led Duke with 30 points, 17 points higher than his average.

The win put Duke in the finals against "Bones" McKinney's Wake Forest Demon Deacons, who were ranked 18th. Wake had defeated Duke by 17 and 19 points in the regular season. Again, Duke's zone baffled its opponent. Wake guards Jerry Ritchie and Billy Packer combined for a miserable 5-27 from the field. Forward Doug Kistler paced Duke with 22 points, including a key jumper that gave Duke a 59-58 lead with 1:40 left. Duke finished the 63-59 win from the foul line.

"It seems like I've always had a horseshoe in these conference tournaments," remarked Bubas, who never lost a Southern Conference Tournament game as a player. "I just decided that I had been over-coaching, that it was time for me to be through with all my experiments."

After the game the exasperated McKinney told Bubas, "Hey, I taught you that defense. I didn't think you'd use it against me."

There was another first associated with the 1960 ACC Tournament. After a seven-inch snowfall made it difficult for some fans to get to North Carolina State's Reynolds Coliseum, Raleigh's WRAL-TV telecast the four first-round games, the first time any ACC Tournament games were on television.

FIRST NCAA WINS

Duke's ACC Tournament win sent them to the NCAA Tournament for only the second time. After an easy opener against Princeton, Duke squared off in the Eastern Regional semifinals against a 22-3 St. Joseph's team. The game was held in Charlotte, the first of many NCAA games Duke has played in its home state. The game had a strange opening. It was being telecast back to the St. Joseph's campus on a closed circuit. The students' cheers were then piped back into the Charlotte Coliseum on loudspeakers. The result was too loud for Vic Bubas' liking, and he had tournament officials turn off the noise.

Duke led 27-20 at the half and extended its lead to 38-27 in the middle of the second half. St. Joseph's was known for its full-court press, and they used this device down the stretch to force turnovers and cut into the Duke lead. With a little more than one minute to go, the lead was down to two points, 56-54. Duke's John Frye and Buzzy Mewhort each made the first end of a one-and-one, but both missed the bonus. Future coaching great Paul Westhead scored for St. Joe's to make the score 58-56 with 20 seconds left.

This set up an ending even more bizarre than the beginning. Frye missed a free throw, giving St. Joseph's a chance to tie. They missed a shot with six seconds left. Duke knocked the ball out of bounds, but the officials didn't stop the clock. The clock ran out before St. Joseph's could get a shot off.

Duke's 58-56 win sent them to the regional finals against New York University, upset winners over Jerry West and West Virginia. Playing their sixth game in nine days, Duke was unable to defend NYU star Tom "Satch" Sanders, who scored 22 points and grabbed 16 rebounds. NYU's 73-59 win ended Duke's surprising season.

Art Heyman

"Looks like I'll have to find a new horseshoe," Bubas quipped after the loss.

ART HEYMAN

Art Heyman was a prep superstar from Long Island. Graduating in 1959, he had been heavily recruited by all of the top programs, Kentucky and Cincinnati among them. However, he was all set to go to the University of North Carolina, whose coach Frank McGuire had established an "Underground Railroad" that funneled New York's top schoolboy talent to Chapel Hill. However, Heyman's stepfather and McGuire did not hit it off. The two men engaged in a fierce shouting match on a recruiting visit when Heyman's stepfather called McGuire's program a "factory." Vic Bubas took over at Duke about the time that UNC was taken off the Heyman table, and he began recruiting Heyman before they could change the coach's name on the office door.

It paid off.

Heyman stunned the basketball world when he signed with Duke. Heyman would be a controversial star. Fiery and flamboyant, he had a temper that erupted both on and off of the court, but his influence on the Duke program is undeniable.

Heyman thought Duke players were too laid back. He went to Bubas and was told to do something about it. Heyman organized preseason workouts that were intense and physical.

"Art kind of opened their eyes as to what it took to be champions," Bubas says. "Of all the players I coached, he was the one I would pick to have the ball at the end of a close game. If he missed the shot, he would get it back. He kept getting the ball back. He had a nose for the basket and was extremely strong. If he got his hands on the ball, it was his. He also was a great passer. He had a great ability to get the ball to the open man."

HANDLING HEYMAN

But how did Vic Bubas handle the legendary Art Heyman temper?

"I loved his fire," Bubas says. "We understood each other. I had to monitor him closely. He was very explosive. The trick was to direct the fire the right way. Sometimes as a coach you had to take certain measures to keep him on track. He always responded the right way."

LET'S GET READY TO RUMBLE

Art Heyman was a 6-foot-5, 205-pound forward. He wasn't a great shooter, but he attacked the basket with a ferocious intensity. In the Dixie Classic during Heyman's sophomore year, North Carolina's equally physical forward Doug Moe put a blanket over Heyman and held him to eight points in a UNC victory. Heyman was determined to exact his revenge in the rematch in Durham. Given Frank McGuire's testy relationship with the Duke fans and the nature of Heyman's recruitment to Duke, it was a highly combustible situation on February 4, 1961.

Not surprisingly it erupted. Heyman was magnificent, scoring 36 points and wrapping up the game with a pair of clutch free throws for an 80-75 lead. UNC's Larry Brown was driving for the basket with nine seconds left when Heyman fouled him hard. Brown came up swinging, UNC's Donnie Walsh joined in, and a full-scale melee was underway. Some 50 players, coaches, and fans were on the floor before the police restored order.

The ACC had been plagued by a rash of fighting, and league commissioner Jim Weaver was determined to put a stop to it. Heyman, Brown, and Walsh were suspended for the remainder of their ACC regular-season games, although a Heyman appeal got his suspension reduced to three games. Duke was 16-1 at the time of the fight but lost its chemistry and ended the season 22-6.

Heyman remains unrepentant.

"I was just protecting myself. Suddenly it seemed like Carolina players were all over me. I was stunned that I was suspended. We never got back into a rhythm. That suspension cost us a national title."

"I never knew Art to start a fight," Vic Bubas adds. "But he sure knew how to finish them."

CHRISTIAN VIRTUES

Art Heyman was one of the first Jewish sports stars in the South. He had to endure anti-Semitic taunts on numerous road trips. Ironically, Heyman once received a letter from the Ku Klux Klan, congratulating him on his adherence to white Christian virtues. Heyman can laugh about it now.

"They couldn't believe that an athlete could be Jewish," he chuckles. "They thought all Jews were tailors or something."

JEFF MULLINS

Art Heyman was the nation's top player by 1963. By then he had been joined by another superstar, junior forward Jeff Mullins. Mullins had grown up in New York state and had gone to high school in Lexington, Kentucky. Adolph Rupp wanted him so badly that he enlisted the efforts of Kentucky governor Bert Coombs, who invited Mullins to the Governor's Mansion for a little man-to-man talk.

"It wasn't as imposing as it sounds," Mullins recalls. "He was very businesslike. He tried to sell me on the advantages I would have after graduation if I stayed in the state. I would have a lot of name recognition and would have lots of business opportunities."

Not many 18-year-olds said no to Rupp in those days, and not many 18-year-olds said no to a governor. Mullins did both.

"I really didn't grow up a Kentucky fan," he explains. "I had only lived in Lexington for a few years."

The previous season Rupp had put a hard sell on Mullins' teammate Jon Speaks, and Mullins didn't like those tactics. Neither did Speaks, who went to North Carolina State.

Vic Bubas had recruited Speaks for State, and Mullins liked what he saw.

"You could tell Bubas was a man on the way up," Mullins says. "Everything about him was impressive."

Mullins was calm and controlled, while Heyman was intense and flamboyant. The two got along well and blended perfectly on the court.

"Not to take anything away from Heyman, but we were always more worried about Mullins," Wake Forest assistant coach Jack Murdock says. "We felt that if we could keep Heyman away from the basket, we could control him. Mullins had more ways to score. He was harder to stop."

Jeff Mullins

PLAYING TOGETHER

In many respects Art Heyman and Jeff Mullins were polar opposites. Heyman was bold and audacious, hot headed on the court, and a playboy off the court. Mullins was quite and methodical, with a Boy Scout's code of conduct. Anyone could have predicted fireworks. Yet, the two got along exceptionally well.

"We had a fine relationship on the court," Mullins says. "We always clicked. It was a win-win situation. I got to play with one of the best players in the country, while Heyman realized that his teammates brought a lot of talent to the team."

Heyman concurs.

"We got along great, on and off the court. Good players want to play with other good players, and Jeff was real good."

LEARNING THE HARD WAY

Duke had an excellent 1962 season, at least until the ACC Tournament. Duke entered the tournament 19-4, ranked eighth in the country and apparently heading for a title match with regular-season champ Wake Forest. Duke overlooked semifinal opponent Clemson and suffered a shocking 77-72 loss to the 11-14 Tigers.

"I learned a valuable lesson from that game," Jeff Mullins laments. "I got all involved with the Wake Forest–South Carolina game held before our game and didn't get mentally prepared for our game. It was a hard lesson to learn, but I never made that mistake again."

A NATURAL RESOURCE

Vic Bubas was a great recruiter, but he didn't get every player he wanted. One of his near misses was Rod Thorn of Princeton, West Virginia. An exceptional student, the 6-foot-3 Thorn wanted to be a doctor, and he was attracted to Duke's prestigious medical school.

So highly regarded was Thorn that the West Virginia legislature passed a resolution naming him a state natural resource. It almost backfired.

"For a while that resolution turned me against going to West Virginia," Thorn said. "But then I realized it was just a nice gesture."

Thorn was inundated with mail from basketball fans across the state, urging him to stay. He finally agreed with them and turned down Bubas.

Thorn never did become a doctor. After an All-America career at West Virginia, he played eight seasons in the NBA and then became an NBA executive. Thorn did make one final trip to Duke. In 1963, his senior year, the sixth-ranked Mountaineers visited the fourth-ranked Blue Devils. Duke buried West Virginia 111-71.

THE ONE WHO GOT AWAY

In the spring of 1961 Washington, D.C.'s Fred Hetzel wanted to take Duke's last scholarship, but Vic Bubas had already given it to a young man named Bill Bradley. Bradley was considered the top high school player in the country, and Duke was going to add to him to a program that already included Art Heyman and Jeff Mullins. On the day that Bradley was supposed to fly in from Missouri for the beginning of the fall semester, Bubas received a phone call from Bradley's father informing him that Bradley was going to Princeton. Ivy League schools didn't participate in the National Letter of Intent program in those days, so Bradley was free to break his commitment to Duke. Bradley, of course, went on to become one of the best college players ever. Hetzel was almost as good at Davidson.

"We really wanted Bradley," Bubas says. "But I was more disappointed in the way that it was handled. I didn't hear from Bill; I heard from his father. Not only did we lose a talented player, but we had saved a scholarship that we could have used on someone else."

Every top program has disappointing near-misses in recruiting, but the circumstances surrounding the loss of Bradley make him Duke's ultimate One Who Got Away.

Bradley played one game against Duke. In December 1962 he scored 24 points in an 85-74 Duke win. The game was played in Durham.

SUMMER VACATIONS

Duke assistant Fred Shabel had been heavily involved in the recruitment of Bill Bradley. Shabel went to Europe for a vacation in the summer of 1961. When he returned, he received a call from Vic Bubas.

"Fred, we lost Bradley. No more summer vacations."

"At first I thought he was joking," Shabel explains. "But he wasn't. He thought that if we had paid more attention to Bradley that summer, he would have come to Duke. The message was clear. Never get outworked. After that, we made sure to keep in contact with our incoming freshmen over the summer. It never happened again."

TELL US WHAT YOU REALLY THINK

Basketball coaches can be highly critical of officials behind closed doors but usually temper their comments in public. But not always. In December 1962 Duke defeated Princeton 85-74. Princeton coach Butch van Breda Kolff blasted the referees.

"You saw what was going on out there. You saw [Art] Heyman pushing and shoving with arms everywhere, and they didn't call the fouls on him. Is that protecting a boy? I like Heyman, but he shouldn't be able to get away with that kind of stuff."

Van Breda Kolff didn't much care for Duke's style of play either.

"Heyman came up to me before the game and said, 'Let's make it a man-to-man game, Coach.' I did, but then they go into a box and one to keep the ball away from [Bill] Bradley. Is that basketball? I came here to see basketball. They didn't want to play basketball; they wanted to stop my man."

SAYING GOODBYE

A senior's final home game can be an emotional moment. Not everyone could handle it. Art Heyman could. Fittingly, his senior-day game was against North Carolina, and Heyman was never better. Vic Bubas gave him the green light.

"Have a little fun," Bubas said. "Do anything you want to."

Heyman responded with 40 points and 24 rebounds to lead Duke to a 106-93 lead. When Bubas took out Heyman at the end of the game, his star put his head under a towel, turned to Bubas, and said, "You know I could have been doing this all the time."

Bubas just smiled.

THE FIRST FINAL FOUR

Art Heyman swept all of the 1963 Player of the Year Awards. Jeff Mullins joined him as All-ACC. The two forwards combined for 45 points and 19 rebounds per game. Mullins excelled in the NCAAs, leading Duke to wins over New York University and St. Joseph's to push Duke to its first Final Four.

Duke was matched against Loyola of Chicago. Vic Bubas made the decision to play to Duke's strengths. Push the ball, fast-break if possible. He quickly had to make a major adjustment. Loyola's quickness on the boards led to several early baskets. Duke quickly fell behind 20-5.

Bubas put Heyman in the backcourt and played a pair of 6-foot-10 players, Jay Buckley and Hack Tison, at the same time. This enabled the Devils to equalize the rebounding battle and slowly climb back into the contest. It was 44-31 at the half, and three Loyola starters had three fouls apiece.

Loyola had to back off in the beginning of the second half because of the foul trouble, and Duke continued to close the gap, led by stalwarts Heyman and Mullins. The gamble worked, as none of the three Loyola players fouled out. With 13:50 to play, Duke was within five points. With eight minutes left it was 65-61, and with 4:20 left, it was 74-71. Then Heyman fouled out, and the Duke gas tank hit empty. Loyola outscored Duke 20-4 down the stretch for a deceptively one-sided final score of 94-75.

Heyman had 29 points and 11 rebounds for Duke. He scored 22 points the next night as Duke defeated Oregon State 85-63 in the consolation game. Heyman was named Most Outstanding Player for the Final Four, a rare honor for a player whose team didn't make the title game. Heyman still feels like this was a missed opportunity.

"We couldn't buy a basket in the first half," he recalls. "Then when we almost caught up, I got called for a foul that could have gone either way and had to sit down. It was a terrible loss. I still think we could have won it all."

A QUIET LEADER

Many fans think that leaders have to be vocal and demonstrative. Not always. Consider Jeff Mullins. Mullins was a quiet leader, a player whose competitiveness might not have been evident to fans in the seats but was obvious to those close to him.

"[He was] a natural leader," Bubas says. "He was a great player and was very popular with his teammates. That doesn't always happen."

His fellow students also recognized these qualities. He was class president at Duke as a sophomore, junior, and senior.

JUST ONE OF THOSE NIGHTS?

Duke went 13-1 in the 1964 ACC regular season and coasted through the 1964 ACC Tournament, winning its games by 31, 16, and 21 points to advance to the Eastern Regionals. The NCAA didn't seed teams in those days. Third-ranked Duke's opener was against seventh-ranked Villanova. Jeff Mullins was never better. He calls it "a special effort. One of those nights." One of those nights was 19-28 from the field, 28 points at intermission and 43 for the game, in an 87-73 Duke win.

Villanova played zone, and Mullins was able to take advantage.

"I just found my way around it," he remembers. "Any zone leaves some holes, and I was able to see them and exploit them."

Mullins punctuated the night with a midcourt buzzer-beater right before halftime. He also shut down Villanova's leading scorer Richie Moore, holding him to eight points.

Mullins scored 30 points in a 101-54 rout of Connecticut in the regional finals. Not surprisingly, he was named Regional Most Outstanding Player. The 47-point win in the finals remains the biggest margin in an NCAA regional title game.

GOING TO KANSAS CITY

The 1964 Final Four was held in Kansas City, Missouri. Wilbert Harrison's "Kansas City" topped the charts that year. It became Duke's unofficial theme song that season. But it wasn't all that it was built up to be. When Duke attempted to fly into Kansas City for the Final, they found that a storm had closed the main airport. They were diverted to a smaller municipal airport. The plane couldn't stop on the smaller runway and slid into the mud, leaving causing plenty of frayed nerves but no lasting problems.

REVENGE IS SWEET

Duke traveled to Ann Arbor, Michigan, early in the 1963-1964 season and came back with a dispiriting 83-67 loss to Michigan. The burly Wolverines, led by 240-pound Bill Buntin and 220-pound Cazzie Russell, bullied Duke much of the game, outrebounding the Devils 61-31. Duke got its chance at revenge in the Final Four.

The key was center Jay Buckley, who had played so poorly in the first game that a North Carolina newspaper referred to him as Duke's "weak link." His bemused teammates called him "Link" for the rest of the season. But not this night.

"[Buckley] played with a mean streak," Mullins recalls. "He popped a few guys in the face early, and we all knew it was going to be different. We took the initiative on the boards."

Buckley scored 25 points and grabbed 14 rebounds as Duke pulled off the 91-80 upset.

THE BRUINS

The physical contest against Michigan took its toll. In those days the NCAA semifinals were held on a Friday, with the title game the following night. Duke had a short time to prepare for an undefeated UCLA team and their potent zone press.

"We put a lot of our eggs in the Michigan basket," Jeff Mullins recalls. "An extra day off might have helped, but UCLA was so good, who knows?"

Duke actually led 30-27 when the Bruins went on a 15-0 run. Duke never climbed back and fell 98-83. Mullins ended his college career with 22 points, giving him 116 points in four NCAA games that season. The win was the first of John Wooden's 10 NCAA titles at UCLA.

13

Jeff Mullins developed one of the most distinctive foul-shooting routines in Duke history. On every foul attempt he would take exactly 13 dribbles, no more, no less. Eventually, the entire Duke student body would count along.

"[I used it] to calm down, to give myself time, to catch my breath after a hard foul," he explains. "I guess it became my signature."

It was an effective routine. Mullins made 76 percent of his free throws at Duke.

SEEING THE WORLD

Jeff Mullins became the first Duke basketball player to participate in the Olympic games, when he made the United States team for the 1964 Tokyo games.

"I can honestly say this was my only long-range goal," he says. "It was a very big deal for me."

Mullins was bothered by tendonitis in his left knee and played sparingly until the semifinal game against Puerto Rico when he scored 14 points, second only to Larry Brown's 16 points. The United States team won a gold medal.

"[I sneaked] into as many events as I could find time to go to," Mullins recalls. "Brown and I had to climb a few fences to see the events we wanted to see, but we weren't going to be stopped."

JACK MARIN

The starting center on Jack Marin's high school team in Farrell, Pennsylvania, was only 5-foot-10. Marin was 6-foot-6, but he played on the perimeter. Was Marin too weak to handle the hard work inside? Hardly. Marin was the team's best ballhandler, best passer, and best outside shot. His high school team couldn't afford to move him inside.

That versatility also sums up Marin's career at Duke. To twist a phrase, Marin was a jack of all trades and a master of most of them.

"[Marin was the] most complete basketball player I've ever coached," Bubas says. "I've had others who could do some things better than Marin, but none as capable as he is when you put them all together. He could find more ways to help us win."

Marin came off the bench for Duke's 1964 team but was an All-ACC forward in 1965 and 1966.

THE HIGHEST SCORING TEAM EVER

Vic Bubas started the 1965 season with a deficit of height but a wealth of talented guards. His decision was to start a trio of backcourters, sophomore Bob Verga, junior Steve Vacendak, and senior Denny Ferguson. None was taller than 6-foot-1. Jack Marin and 6-foot-10 Hack Tison patrolled the inside.

Vacendak made it work. Literally. He scrapped and fought against bigger and taller men to the tune of 6.6 rebounds per game. Marin, Verga, and Vacendak could all run and shoot. They combined for almost 60 points per game. Without benefit of either a shot clock or a three-point shot, the 1965 team averaged 92.4 points per game, setting a school record that has not been equaled. In February Duke blasted Virginia 136-72, still the most points scored in one game in Duke history.

Duke captured its third consecutive regular-season crown and entered the ACC Tournament as two-time defending champions. Unfortunately, Duke ran into a buzz saw in the finals. Unheralded North Carolina State forward Larry Worsley hit 14 of 19 field goals, mostly from long range, and scored 30 points, 25 over his average. Duke fell to the Wolfpack 91-85 and ended their season at 20-5.

Bubas still has thoughts of what might have been.

"I think we were poised to do some real damage in the NCAAs," Bubas laments. "We had been to the Final Four the two previous seasons, and we liked the feeling. We wanted to go back."

THE BRUINS GO DOWN

The 1965-1966 Duke team started the season ranked No. 3 in the AP poll, trailing two-time defending national champions UCLA and Michigan. Both the Bruins and the Wolverines were on Duke's schedule for December 1965. In fact, UCLA was on it twice. Vic Bubas and John Wooden had agreed to play two games in North Carolina, the first at Duke and the second in Charlotte. UCLA had defeated Duke for the 1964 NCAA title, but the two programs had not played in the regular season since 1953.

Duke won both games easily, 82-66 and 94-75, neutralizing UCLA's vaunted zone press and controlling the paint. Sophomore center Mike Lewis dominated the first game, with 21 points and 16 rebounds, while Jack Marin's 23 points and Bob Verga's 22 points paced Duke in the second game.

"Duke just ripped us," Wooden responded, "and when you get whipped, well, you just get whipped."

As a result of the two wins, Duke jumped to No. 1 in the AP and UPI polls, the first time the program had ever topped either poll.

Ironically, Duke had begun the week with a loss to South Carolina. Duke is probably the only team to ever ascend to No. 1 in the polls in a week following a loss.

Before the first game Bubas invited Wooden with him to visit Bubas' old college coach, North Carolina State legend Everett Case. Wooden and Case knew each other from their days in Indiana. Bubas mainly listened to the two exchange war stories. Six months later Case was dead from cancer.

COMING FROM BEHIND

Duke played Michigan in less hospitable surroundings. The result of their December 21, 1965 matchup was one of the great comebacks in school history. Duke still was ranked No. 1 in the polls but Cazzie Russell's Wolverines were ranked third. The game was held in nearby Detroit rather than Ann Arbor. Led by Russell, who would score 30 points on the night, Michigan jumped to a 49-41 halftime lead. They extended the lead to 55-41.

Teams as good as Michigan was rarely relinquish 14-point leads in the second half in front of a partisan crowd, but the 1965-1966 Duke team was no ordinary opponent. A 9-0 Duke run ate into the Michigan lead, but a spurt by the home team extended the lead back to 10 with only four minutes remaining. Bob Riedy and Mike Lewis muscled inside for a pair of three-point plays. Duke eventually took an 85-83 lead, but Michigan's John Clawson followed a missed shot at the buzzer to send the game into overtime.

The two exhausted teams traded baskets early in the overtime before Duke pulled away. Verga scored nine of Duke's final 11 points as the Devils pulled off a pulsating 100-93 win. Marin matched Russell's 30 points, while Verga added 27, 20 after intermission. Vic Bubas called the game "the greatest comeback any Duke team has ever staged."

STEVE VACENDAK

Steve Vacendak was a tough, heady guard. The six-foot-one Scranton native was so hard-nosed that he started at forward in 1965 and pulled down almost seven rebounds per game.

Bucky Waters recruited Vacendak to Duke. He tells the story of the first time he saw Vacendak.

"He was maybe 6-foot-1 guarding some 6-foot-6 kid who looked like a tight end. Steve just beat the guy into submission. He was that tough."

Later Duke was evaluating potential recruits. Vic Bubas asked Waters about Vacendak.

"I'd take him," Waters said.

"Really," Bubas asked. "Is he a good shooter?"

"I don't know," Waters answered.

"Is he a good ballhandler?" Bubas continued.

"I'm not real sure," Waters responded.

"Well, what do you see in him?"

"Vic, he's too small to play center, but he does," the Duke assistant said. "He made 1200 on his SAT, he's tough as nails, and if anybody plays ahead of him, then we're real good."

Waters turned out to be right.

PLAYER OF THE YEAR

Back at his natural guard position in 1966, Steve Vacendak figured in one of the more bizarre awards in basketball annals. Duke dominated the league that year and received the expected rewards. The ACC sportswriters named Jack Marin and Bob Verga first-team All-ACC, while national writers and coaches selected both for numerous All-America squads. Vacendak was named second-team All-ACC, finishing ninth in the voting.

Not everyone agreed with that assessment.

"How in the world could anybody pick an all-conference team and leave off Steve Vacendak?" Clemson coach Bobby Roberts argued. "As far as I'm concerned he's the best boy in the league. He's the heart and soul of the Duke team."

The writers began to rethink their position in the ACC Tournament, held days after the All-ACC team was announced. The heady Vacendak held Duke together in the face of Dean Smith's Four Corners as Duke defeated UNC 21-20 in the semifinals. He made several key baskets down the stretch as Duke came from behind to edge North Carolina State 71-66 in the title game. Vacendak led Duke with 18 points, including eight in the final 4:28. Vic Bubas praised his senior.

"He's the best battler that we've had since I've been at Duke," he said. "There's no doubt in my mind who leaves the most out there all the time."

Not surprisingly, Vacendak was awarded the Everett Case Trophy as the tournament's outstanding player. More surprisingly, the same sportswriters who had placed Vacendak ninth in the All-ACC voting the week before the tournament voted him Atlantic Coast Conference Player of the Year the week after the tournament. He received 51 votes, with teammate Marin a distant second with 29 votes. Vacendak remains the only player in ACC history to pull off this unlikely combination.

SETTING THE PACE

Steve Vacendak set the tone for the Duke team as its leader.

"If there was a loose ball, he would get it," Mike Lewis recalls. "If we needed someone to take the last shot, he would take it. His attitude was give me the damn ball and get out of the way."

Vacendak did some of his best work in practice.

"I had never seen anyone work so hard in practice," says Lewis, a sophomore in 1966. "He never took a second off, never took a play off. I figured this was the way champions were made. If a senior, the captain, was going to bust his ass in practice every day like that, I knew I couldn't play half-assed."

BOB VERGA

Bob Verga may have been the best pure shooter in Duke history. He had great range and the conscience of a thief. If he was past midcourt, he was open.

"Sure Bob shot all the time, but that was what he was supposed to do," teammate Mike Lewis recalls. "He did it better than anyone else in the country, so why should we put restraints on him?"

Verga was a newspaperman's dream. He drove a Corvette Sting Ray, dated a model, and always seemed to be on the go.

"This was all exaggerated," Lewis confesses. "Verga actually was something of a loner. He didn't hang out with the rest of the guys. But it made great copy."

Bob Verga

HOLDING THE BALL

In the late 1960s Duke was big, deep, and talented. Teams that weren't big, deep, and talented eventually decided that their best bet to beat Duke was to hold the ball, shorten the game, and force Duke to chase. With no shot clock, there was nothing to stop teams from attempting this strategy.

The first to employ this tactic was Duke's old nemesis, Frank McGuire. On Valentine's Day 1966, McGuire's South Carolina Gamecocks came to Durham. Duke was vulnerable that night. Bob Verga was serving the second game of a two-game suspension. The first game was for violating curfew; the second was for questioning Vic Bubas. Duke led only 26-20 at the half. Led by the clutch play of Steve Vacendak, Duke held off South Carolina 41-38. The 79 total points was the lowest in a Duke game since UNC defeated Duke 49-28 in 1947, but it would be the beginning of a trend.

Not surprisingly there were fireworks. At intermission McGuire was bending the ear of referee Curly White. Bubas came over to get in his two cents' worth. McGuire emphatically told Bubas to get out of the way and mind his own business. The two coaching giants continued an animated exchange for several minutes before going to their locker rooms.

After the game McGuire explained his strategy.

"It was the only thing I could do. It was our only chance to win here. If we run with Duke, they'd score 120 points. We'd be lucky to get 60."

DEEP FREEZE 1

The South Carolina game was only a prelude. Duke would be involved in some memorable slow-down games. Later that 1966 season Duke took a 20-3 mark and a No. 2 national ranking into an ACC Tournament semifinal match against the University of North Carolina. Dean Smith was one year away from his first Final Four team. His team had lost twice to Duke already that season 88-77 and 77-63. Smith decided to have his team spread the court and hold the ball. Duke stayed back in a zone. The result was a 7-5 Duke lead at halftime.

"We had no idea something like this was coming," Mike Lewis says. "We thought that UNC wasn't good enough to play that way without making some mistakes. Then we would get them down, force them to run, and beat them badly."

UNC extended their lead to 17-12 before Duke fought back. Steve Vacendak tied the game 20-20 with a jumper with about two minutes left. UNC missed a free throw with 1:40 left. Duke rebounded and held for the last shot. Lewis was fouled with four seconds left. Lewis wasn't concerned. At least until a teammate walked by.

"We really need these," he whispered.

"Like I didn't know that," Lewis recalls. "Still, I really wasn't too worried. I knew I was a good foul shooter. I was pretty sure I could make one of two. Then I choked on the first one and the rim got a little smaller. Actually, it got a lot smaller. By that time I was so nervous I didn't even know if my knees were knocking or not."

Nervous or not, Lewis made the second foul shot. Duke won 21-20 and captured the ACC title the following night.

Smith was unapologetic.

"I thought we deserved victory. We had tried to go up and down with them twice and lost."

Vic Bubas was terse.

"I have no comment on their style of play. It's in the rulebook, and a coach can elect to use it. That's his decision."

A BAD TIME TO GET SICK

Vic Bubas has long maintained that the 1966 team was his best. It's easy to see why. Bob Verga and Jack Marin were All-Americans. Mike Lewis and Bob Riedy provided size and rebounding. Steve Vacendak was the ballhandler and leader. The bench was solid. The team could shoot, rebound, and defend.

It also was battle tested. A brutal non-conference schedule prepared Duke for the ACC. Duke went 13-1 in the regular season but still had to capture the conference tournament. Close wins over rivals North Carolina and North Carolina State sent Duke to the Eastern Regionals where Duke outlasted old rival St. Josephs 76-74. A 91-81 win over Dave Bing and Syracuse sent Duke to its third Final Four in four seasons.

With a title in sight, disaster struck. Verga came down with strep throat and a bronchial infection. Even with a fever in excess of 100 degrees, Duke's leading scorer gamely tried to go against the Kentucky

Wildcats. But it was a futile gesture. He could score only four points in 21 minutes, and Duke fell 83-79.

Bubas can't resist the temptation to think about what might have been.

"I compare it to having Mickey Mantle on the bench just because he's banged up. We were going to play Verga. You'll never know for sure, but I think we would have won with a healthy Verga. We all felt like we could have won it all. But it's just speculation. You have to be ready on the right day."

Verga's fever broke the next day. He scored 15 points in a consolation win over Utah.

(In those days the Final Four was played on Friday and Saturday. Had the schedule been Saturday and Monday, as it is today, Verga might have been well enough to lead Duke to the title.)

DEEP FREEZE 2

Duke survived the stalls of 1966. Two years later they weren't so fortunate. Ranked sixth in the nation, Duke met an overmatched North Carolina State team in the ACC Tournament semifinals. State coach Norm Sloan, a former teammate of Vic Bubas' at North Carolina State, ordered his team to hold the ball.

Bubas steadfastly refused to allow his team to chase the smaller but quicker State players. The result was almost surreal. State led 4-2 at the half. UNC radio announcer Bill Currie shocked his audience by declaring the game "about as exciting as artificial insemination." Duke jumped to an 8-6 lead early in the second half and then retreated back into its zone. State's Bill Kretzer then spent an astonishing 13 minutes dribbling the ball alone near midcourt, occasionally tossing the ball to a teammate to relieve the boredom. Once State's Eddie Biedenbach went over to the sidelines to consult with Sloan during the "action." Duke's Tony Barone went over and theatrically listened in before Sloan shooed him away. Angry fans threw pennies on the floor, prompting referee Otis Almond to quip, "It's always pennies, never quarters."

Action resumed with about three minutes left. State regained the lead amidst a flurry of Duke turnovers and missed free throws. With six seconds left, Duke's Dave Golden went to the foul line with his team trailing 11-9. Golden made his first foul shot but missed the second.

State grabbed the rebound and made the final free throw for a 12-10 win.

Sloan echoed Smith's comments of two seasons before.

"We have no reservations about playing that way. We played to win."

"We're a big team, and we're not suited to pressing," Bubas admitted. "They probably would have won if he had come out and chased them."

"[It was] my worst loss ever, nothing else is even close," Mike Lewis recalls 40 years later. "I was so devastated I didn't even want to get out of my uniform and take a shower. It was such a bad feeling that I can't even begin to describe it."

SENDING A MESSAGE

Duke traveled to Los Angeles early in the 1966-1967 season to play a pair of games against UCLA. Duke had defeated the Bruins twice the previous season in games played in North Carolina. Some fans directed racial slurs at the UCLA players. The Bruins were led by sophomore sensation Lew Alcindor, who had not played in the previous year's contests.

"They were waiting for us," Mike Lewis remembers. "They wanted to beat us big time."

"Before the first game we were warming up on the other end of the court while UCLA was warming up in front of our bench," Vic Bubas recalls. "Alcindor went in for a layup and came running back to the end of the layup line. This was near where I was standing. He turned toward me and gave me a grin that went from ear to ear. I turned to one of my assistants and said, 'We're in a hell of a fix.'"

Bubas was right. UCLA won 88-54 and 107-87, as Alcindor scored 57 points, with 38 rebounds in the two games. The losses dropped Duke out of the AP top 10 for the first time since 1960.

A COSTLY NIGHT OUT

Duke ended 1966 on a down note. Playing in a tournament in Greensboro, Duke lost to Ohio State by a point and defeated Wake Forest by five. They entered 1967 with an uncharacteristic 4-4 record. They also entered 1967 with an uncharacteristic problem. Fans at the first game of the new year, against Penn State, were shocked when only seven players took the court for Duke. Shortly before game time Vic Bubas announced that he had suspended indefinitely nine players, including four starters.

Mike Lewis was one of the suspended players.

"We had gone out drinking at the local Holiday Inn," he explains. "I guess somebody saw us and blew the whistle. Bubas confronted us. You've got two choices in a situation like that. You can lie and try to brazen it out, or you can be a man about it, tell the truth, and take the consequences. We told the truth. Coach had rules, and we broke them and accepted our fate. He was right, and we were wrong."

EMPTYING THE BENCH

The only starter not suspended for the Penn State game was star guard Bob Verga. Former walk-on Stu McKaig joined him in the starting lineup. Three little-used sophomores, Fred Lind, Steve Vandenberg, and C.B. Claiborne were the frontcourt starters. Two walk-ons comprised the bench. Vic Bubas even approached football All-America linebacker Bob Matheson about playing. Matheson agreed to dress out at halftime if Bubas needed him.

Surprisingly, Bubas didn't need him. Verga poured in 23 points before intermission and sparked Duke to a 51-41 lead. Verga hit his first five field goal attempts in the second half, and Duke built the lead. All of the starters except Lind went the entire 40 minutes. As fatigue inevitably set in, Penn State ate into the margin. Verga made four clutch free throws in the last minute, and Duke held on for an improbable 89-84 victory. Verga ended with 38 points, while Vandenberg provided the inside balance with 16 points.

"It wasn't something we dwelled on," Bubas says. "It happened, and we moved on."

He reinstated seven players for the next game but held out starter Bob Riedy because it was his second offense. Riedy's loss was crucial, as Duke lost 59-56 to North Carolina.

C.B. CLAIBORNE

Claudius B. Claiborne was an outstanding student and basketball player at Danville, Virginia's John M. Langston High School. He was all set to go to the North Carolina A&T State when he received a National Achievement Scholarship, which enabled him to attend

Bob Verga and Vic Bubas

Duke. Claiborne was the first African-American athlete at Duke, the third African-American player in the ACC, and the first African-American basketball player in the Big Four. The six-foot-two Claiborne played sparingly at Duke until his senior season, 1968-1969, when he started several games and averaged more than six points per game.

Vic Bubas played with and against black players in high school in Gary, Indiana.

"I never had direct orders not to recruit black players," he explains, "but it was generally understood that we had to wait until the time was right. When C.B. came along, we knew he was the right guy. Eddie Cameron was totally supportive."

Claiborne went on to earn several graduate degrees, including a doctorate in marketing.

BAD BLOOD

Frank McGuire left North Carolina for the NBA but returned to the ACC in 1964 as head coach at South Carolina. It didn't take long for McGuire to renew his feud with Duke. The catalyst for the worst McGuire–Duke feud was Mike Grosso, a 6-foot-9 center from New Jersey. The ACC in those days required a minimum SAT score of 800 for an athletic scholarship. Grosso just missed. His family supposedly paid his way, but Eddie Cameron heard otherwise. Cameron and UNC athletic director Chuck Erickson complained to the ACC. The league investigated Grosso and determined that he had received illegal aid. In October 1966 the ACC ruled him ineligible. South Carolina threatened lawsuits, threatened to leave the ACC, and went through several unsuccessful appeals. Grosso never played a varsity game for South Carolina and transferred to Louisville.

McGuire took this as a personal affront. Shortly after Grosso was ruled ineligible, McGuire complained, "This thing is being directed at me and taken out on the boy."

The gloves came off completely in a speech in Charlotte in late November.

"This is a spite vendetta in which two athletic directors are trying to stop me. I have never gotten into the gutter with the skunks before in my life, but this time I have. I'm not doing this for myself but to save a boy's life. We have a game with Duke on December 19.

Apparently, they will put this thing off until they can find a reason not to play us."

A quarter-century later McGuire wrote in his book *Frank McGuire: The Life and Times of a Basketball Legend,* "Eddie Cameron ... seemed to have a personal vendetta against us, and he waged a campaign to have Mike declared ineligible.... As far as I am concerned it made a victim out of an innocent boy and a fine athlete mainly because of my relationship with Eddie Cameron and Duke."

The blood was so bad that the ACC gave Duke and UNC the opportunity to cancel both of their 1967 regular-season matches with South Carolina. Duke accepted the offer, citing the need for a "cooling-off period."

As fate would have it, Duke and South Carolina met in the 1967 ACC Tournament semifinals. Both Vic Bubas and McGuire kept a tight rein on their teams, and the expected rumble never happened. Duke won a close contest 69-66. North Carolina defeated Duke the next night for the title.

NIT

For more than a decade into its existence the ACC refused to allow its teams to play in the National Invitation Tournament in New York.

"It was just conservatism, just inertia," Vic Bubas says. "The NIT was bigger in those days. It was important to play the extra games, to gain some extra exposure. I thought the league was short-changing itself. I lobbied hard to have that policy changed."

Bubas' efforts paid off in 1967, when the ACC voted to change its policy. Duke was the first ACC team to receive and accept a bid to the NIT. The timing was awful, however. The NIT began play the same day that Duke lost to North Carolina in the ACC Tournament finals. The ACC runner-up, which turned out to be Duke, received a bye into the second round. Duke played Southern Illinois and Walt Frazier two days later and lost 72-63. It was Duke's fourth game in five days. Southern Illinois went on to win the NIT.

"It was too soon," Mike Lewis says. "We were still mourning not winning the ACC Tournament when we had to get on a plane and fly to New York. We were tired and frustrated. Most of us didn't want to be there. If we had a few days to think about it, to get ourselves together mentally, I think we could have won the whole thing. But not the way it was set up."

MIKE LEWIS

Duke has recruited players from some out-of-the-way places but few more out of the way than Montana's Mike Lewis. Lewis recalls Duke assistant Bucky Waters making a recruiting visit.

"It wasn't easy getting from Durham to Missoula. You had to change planes about a dozen times. One time Waters came in after a particularly stormy flight, looking a little green and a little unsteady. He took one look at me and said, 'Damn, you better be good.'"

YOU CAN LEAVE NOW

Bucky Waters didn't do all the recruiting, of course. One time Vic Bubas visited Mike Lewis and immediately asked Lewis and his brother to take a walk, so he could talk to the parents.

"I don't know what they said," Lewis recalls, "but after Bubas left, my father told me, 'Son, this is the man you want to play basketball for.' My dad wasn't a real social person, but he was a great judge of character. He was rarely wrong, and he wasn't wrong then."

RUSTIC MOUNTAIN MAN?

It's tempting to look at the burly Mike Lewis as some sort of untutored mountain force of nature. His nickname at Duke was the "Missoula Moose." Nothing could be further from the truth. Missoula County High School had more than 2,000 students. Lewis was coached by Lou Rouchleau, a former University of Montana star. They won several state titles. Lewis was also a Parade All-American.

"When I got to Duke they introduced us to some basic rebounding drills," Lewis recalls. "I told the coaches I don't need this crap. I've been doing this stuff since the 10th grade."

REBOUNDING

Mike Lewis was one of the great rebounders in ACC history. He led the league in 1966 and 1968 and finished second in 1967.

"At first that was my primary responsibility," Lewis explains. "Get inside, do the dirty work, and come away with the basketball. It didn't have to be pretty, just effective."

Gradually, Lewis refined his offensive game. In 1968, his senior year he averaged almost 22 points per game.

THREE OVERTIMES

Mike Lewis' final home game was one of the great games in Duke history. Duke was ranked 10th and North Carolina was ranked third when they came to Durham on March 2, 1968. Lewis had a bittersweet finale. He had an exceptional game, scoring 18 points and pulling down an equal number of rebounds. However, he fouled out with 3:54 left and Duke trailing by three. He was replaced by little-used reserve Fred Lind, who was averaging about one point per game. Lind responded with 16 points, nine rebounds, and several key defensive plays.

He made two free throws to send the game into overtime and a late jump shot that sent the game into its second overtime. Duke won 87-86 in three overtimes.

"It was agonizing watching from the bench," Lewis says. "I felt like I was letting my team down. Then it occurred to me that I couldn't possibly do any better than Freddie was doing. So I sat back and tried to enjoy it."

"Like all reserves, I was sure I could play if I just had the chance," Lind confesses. "I had been waiting a long time for a chance like that. I worked hard in practice, stayed in shape, and tried to be ready. Coach [Vic] Bubas told me I would probably play against Carolina because of their size, so I had a suspicion. I was so busy I didn't have time to be nervous. Besides I had been practicing against Mike Lewis for two years. What could UNC do to me that he hadn't already done?"

ABE LEMONS

Duke's 12-10 loss to North Carolina State in the ACC Tournament sent the Devils to the NIT for the second year.

"I didn't want to go," Lewis recalls. "If I could have paid someone to take my place, I would have."

Duke opened against Oklahoma City, coached by Abe Lemons, a legendary wit. The teams stayed in the same hotel, and Lewis actually rode in the elevator with Lemons.

"By the time we hit the ground floor and the door opened, I felt like I had gone nine floors with Bob Hope. He was the funniest man I ever met."

SHIRTS VERSUS SKINS

Duke led Oklahoma City 49-28 at the half. Oklahoma City's first-half performance was so dismal that Abe Lemons refused to let his players go to the locker room. Instead he kept them on the court for an impromptu shirts versus skins scrimmage that lasted until the bemused Duke team came back on the floor.

Lemons explained the strange behavior.

"We're just a bunch of country boys, and this big city stuff scares us. None of us got any sleep last night. I thought maybe we could get comfortable if we stayed out a little longer."

The game got even stranger. With about two minutes left, a fight broke out behind the Duke bench involving a couple of intoxicated hecklers. A policeman tried to stop the fight and was pushed into the scorer's table, breaking the table and disabling the clock. Lemons pleaded for the officials to end the one-sided game but to no avail. After a lengthy delay, the decision was made to hand-time the final minutes. The game mercifully ended with Duke ahead 97-81.

Duke lost to local favorite St. Peter's in the next game 100-71. Duke was plagued with foul trouble. Mike Lewis picked up three fouls in the first two minutes and played only 12 minutes before fouling out.

"I didn't need to take a shower after that one," Lewis quips. "I hadn't been in the game long enough to work up a sweat."

THE KILLER VERSUS THE KING

Forward Steve Vandenberg had a hobby. He could play a mean boogie-woogie piano. He put together a combo and played shows on campus, specializing in the music of "The Killer," Jerry Lee Lewis.

"We used to get into arguments with him all the time," Lewis remembers. "Bobo [Bob Riedy] would maintain that Elvis was the greatest, and Steve would counter with Jerry Lee. I had to side with Bobo. How could you not know that Elvis was the greatest of all time? But Steve would never back down."

SAYING GOODBYE

In mid-February Vic Bubas informed his Duke team that he was retiring from coaching at the conclusion of the season. Duke responded with a 122-93 blitzing of Wake Forest. The news didn't stay secret for long. Duke ended its regular season at home against second-ranked North Carolina. Bubas played a hunch and started senior forward Steve Vandenberg, a former starter who had lost his starting position because of lackluster play. He was averaging only six points per game.

Vandenberg responded in sterling fashion. He made 10 of 14 field goals and all 13 free throws for 33 points and added a dozen rebounds. Duke led 46-33 at the half, fell behind briefly after intermission, but pulled away down the stretch for an 87-81 win.

"We really didn't have any squad meeting or pep talks before the game," Vandenberg says. "It wasn't the way we did things. We knew what was at stake. We decided to just go out and play."

ONE LAST TIME

Duke came close to sending off Vic Bubas in style. Bubas decided to compress his rotation for the ACC Tournament, giving the bulk of the minutes to seniors Steve Vandenberg, Fred Lind, and Dave Golden and sophomores Randy Denton and Dick DeVenzio. Bubas only played six players in a first-round victory over Virginia.

Duke advanced to a semifinal match against Frank McGuire's South Carolina Gamecocks. McGuire rarely used his bench, and his 1969 bench scored a mere 71 points over the entire season. South Carolina had defeated Duke twice in the regular season and was poised for a sweep that would send them into the tournament finals against North Carolina.

There was no love lost between Duke and McGuire, and the last meeting between Bubas and McGuire was close and physical. Incredibly, each of the 10 starters played the entire 40 minutes. Duke held South Carolina star John Roche to a four of 15 shooting night, but the Gamecocks stayed close behind 19-of-20 foul shooting. On defense and trailing 60-59 in the last minute, South Carolina had committed only three team fouls, well short of the minimum seven that would require Duke to go to the foul line. DeVenzio was fouled three times in short order. The third was so obvious that an intentional foul was called. DeVenzio made both free throws, and Vandenberg got loose on the subsequent inbounds pass. The four-point possession keyed Duke to a 68-59 win.

LAST GAME

Duke was matched against heavily favored North Carolina for the ACC title. Duke was superb. Randy Denton scored 19 points and pulled down 11 rebounds. The other four Duke starters scored in double figures. Duke led 43-34 at intermission and still led by 11 points in the middle of the second half. At that point Charlie Scott took over. The North Carolina All-American scored 28 points after intermission.

"I kept trying to contest Charlie's shots, but I kept having to turn around and pick the ball out of the net," Denton explains.

Scott ended with 40 points, and UNC came back for an 85-74 win. Duke ended the season 15-13.

"We tried everything we could," Vic Bubas says. "Scott was just too good, truly unstoppable."

WHY RETIRE?

A few weeks before the end of the season Vic Bubas had stunned the basketball world by announcing that he would retire at the end of the 1969 season at age 42.

"The thought of getting on another plane and chasing another high school kid was just overwhelming," Bubas explains. "Toward the end I took longer to dress for practice. You wonder should you see one more film, one more kid? At the end, it wasn't fair to the kids, wasn't fair to the team. It was time to do something else."

Randy Denton remembers how he learned of Bubas' plans.

"He called us into his office, one at a time. He told us that he had lost his passion and that it wasn't fair for anyone to continue like that."

Bubas worked as an administrator at Duke until 1976, when he became the first commissioner of the Sunbelt Conference, a position he held until 1990. His final record at Duke was an extraordinary 213-67.

Chapter 4
THE UP AND DOWN 1970s

BUCKY WATERS

Bucky Waters is the most controversial coach in Duke history. Waters had been an assistant at Duke under Vic Bubas before leaving to become head coach at West Virginia. He had success at Morgantown, including a 1966 win over the top-ranked Blue Devils. He replaced Bubas at Duke.

The move made sense at the time. He knew the school, and he knew the program. Waters was only 32 years old, but Eddie Cameron and Bubas had been about the same age when they took over the reins at Duke. Waters' first two Duke teams went 17-9 and 20-10, both improvements over Bubas' last team. But disgruntled players began to transfer, and by his third season Waters was under fire.

RANDY DENTON

The best gift Vic Bubas left Bucky Waters was Randy Denton, a 6-foot-11, 250-pound center. Denton was from Raleigh and was one of Bubas' few top recruits from North Carolina. Denton led Duke in scoring and rebounding in three varsity seasons at Duke, an accomplishment matched only by Art Heyman and Danny Ferry. He averaged 19.7 points per game for his career at Duke, while his 12.7 rebounds per game is the best in school history.

COMING TO DUKE

North Carolina coach Dean Smith pretty much had his way in recruiting North Carolina during the 1960s. Randy Denton was one of the few who got away. Duke had a secret weapon in recruiting Denton. Denton went to Enloe High School in Raleigh. His high school coach, Howard Hurt, had starred at Duke, making All-ACC in 1959, 1960, and 1961.

"Hurt made me his special project," Denton explains. "He worked with me during the summer, worked me into shape. He made sure I knew what it would take to make it at the college level. He also made sure I knew about Duke and how he felt about Vic Bubas."

By 1967 Denton was one of the nation's top prep centers. Denton's father, Allan, passed away in Randy's junior year at Enloe. Allan Denton had wanted his son to go to Duke, and Denton honored his father's wish, picking Duke over UNC.

BE A BULLY?

Randy Denton was a gentle giant.

"Randy was a reluctant star," Bucky Waters recalls. "Like many big kids, he had been raised not to be a bully. We kept asking ourselves what we could do to make him mad and keep him mad. Sometimes we wished he would be more selfish."

Denton agrees. "That's probably an accurate assessment. That's the way I am."

BEATING THE BEST

Randy Denton had little trouble getting motivated to play against other top centers. As a sophomore he outplayed Western Kentucky's Jim McDaniels to lead Duke to the Sugar Bowl championship. In his junior year Denton scored 27 points and pulled down a dozen rebounds in a Duke win against Rudy Tomjanovich and Michigan. In the Kentucky Invitational against the top-ranked Wildcats, Denton dominated All-American Dan Issel, scoring 28 points and pulling down 21 rebounds in a losing cause.

"Randy put on a clinic against Issel," Bucky Waters says, "just destroyed him."

Later that season Denton had a 25-point, 13-rebound performance against Davidson's Mike Maloy as Duke upset the ninth-ranked Wildcats.

"For some reason I was always focused against the top big men," Denton confesses. "I didn't want to embarrass myself. I couldn't always bring the same intensity to every game, unfortunately."

DICK DeVENZIO

One of Randy Denton's classmates was Dick DeVenzio, a heady point guard from Pennsylvania. The two even roomed together for a season. Almost a foot shorter than Denton, DeVenzio was quick and skilled. Writers spent three years making Mutt and Jeff analogies for Denton and DeVenzio.

"Dick was the most intense guy I ever played with," Denton recalls. "He was intense about class, he was intense about practice, he was really intense about games. He would sing the Duke fight song before going to sleep."

DeVenzio loved playing up-tempo basketball. He averaged more than 12 points per game as sophomore under Vic Bubas, including a 28-point outburst against powerful Davidson. Bucky Waters slowed down the tempo and reined in his point guard. DeVenzio chafed under the restrictions. Injuries further hampered his final two years.

But DeVenzio stuck it out.

"He really loved Duke's academics," Denton explains, "and he wanted the Duke degree."

DeVenzio later wrote five instructional books and became a noted basketball tutor. He also became a vociferous advocate for college athletes, arguing that they were exploited and deserved to be paid for their efforts. He died of cancer in 2001 at age 52.

"If he could," his father noted after his son's death, "he'd still tell you the NCAA people are all a bunch of crooks."

WHAT HAPPENED?

Bucky Waters' first two Duke teams had better records than Vic Bubas' last Duke squad did, but they were plagued by inconsistency. Impressive wins would be followed with perplexing losses. In both the 1970 and 1971 seasons, Duke ended the regular campaign with wins over highly ranked North Carolina, only to fall in the opening round of the ACC Tournament.

Randy Denton remains baffled.

"Obviously we weren't ready to play. But that's hindsight. We had good practices, we thought we were ready, and we took the floor expecting to win. Then, nothing happened. We just didn't have it."

Duke advanced to the NIT both seasons, finishing fourth in 1971.

AN UNEXPECTED HERO

Duke renamed Duke Indoor Stadium Cameron Indoor Stadium, in honor of retiring athletic director and former coach Eddie Cameron on January 22, 1972. The dedication game was against a second-ranked North Carolina team, which included future NBA stars Robert McAdoo and Bobby Jones. Duke center Alan Shaw harassed McAdoo into a one-of-12 shooting nightmare, while Duke forwards Richie O'Conner and Chris Redding each scored 24 points.

Still the game was tied 74-74 with a few seconds left, with Duke in possession. Robbie West had the ball near midcourt. West wouldn't have been Duke's first choice for this situation. A senior guard, West had scored less than 100 points for his entire Duke career up to that point. This was only his fifth start at Duke. But West dribbled to about 20 feet from the basket and calmly buried a jump shot. The Duke students rushed the floor, but the officials cleared the court, put three seconds back on the clock, and resumed play. A hurried shot by Dennis Wuycik missed the mark, and Duke had the win.

After the game West clinically dissected the game-winner.

"When my shot leaves my hand, I can just about tell what it will do. When that one left, I knew it was good. It felt smooth when it rolled off my fingertips. I've always felt like I could play, if I got the chance. Today, I got the chance."

Ironically, West's parents had planned to come from New Jersey to watch the game in person, but his mother came down with the flu, and they stayed home. The game wasn't televised in New Jersey, either.

THE GAME BALL

The combination of Robbie West's last-minute shot and the Cameron dedication provided a great photo-op. West presented the game ball to Eddie Cameron after the game. A few days later he repeated the act for photographers. Then a third time at the team's basketball banquet.

"They can keep giving me that ball as long as they want, as long as they don't change the final score," Cameron quipped.

GARY MELCHIONNI

When Gary Melchionni was 13 years old, his family made its first trip to Tobacco Road. The Melchionnis were at North Carolina State's Reynolds Coliseum to see Melchionni's older brother, Bill, and his Villanova teammates play Duke in the 1964 Eastern Regionals. Villanova lost 87-73, but Melchionni was intrigued by his first exposure to Duke basketball.

Five years later, Melchionni was a high school standout in New Jersey. Another older brother, Bob, had joined Bill at Villanova. Younger brother Tom would eventually become a Wildcat. Yet Villanova waffled on offering Gary a scholarship. Duke didn't waffle at all, and Bucky Waters signed perhaps the top recruit in his tenure at Duke.

A gifted 6-foot-3 left-handed guard, Melchionni struggled at first with injuries and illness, including a bout with mononucleosis. He began to put it together in the middle of his junior year. An academic All-American, Melchionni was a gifted shooter, ballhandler, and defender. After Duke upset second-ranked North Carolina in 1972, Tar Heels coach Dean Smith praised Melchionni.

"He was tremendous. Duke was hard to stop after they got the ball inbounds. He just broke our press."

Melchionni ended his Duke career in 1973 as a first-team All-ACC guard.

"THE MONGOOSE"

The highlight of Gary Melchionni's career came in February 1973, his senior year, when Duke hosted third-ranked Maryland. Lefty Driesell's Terps were loaded that year, with Tom McMillen, John Lucas, and Len Elmore. At this point Duke was running a spread offense, which Bucky Waters dubbed "The Mongoose." Typically, Melchionni would have the ball in the middle of the court, with the option to drive, pull up for a shot, or pass. "The Mongoose" never looked better than it did against Maryland. Melchionni out-quicked the big guys, overpowered the quick guys, and baffled the Terps all night. He ended up with 39 points, on 17 of 25 shooting from the field and five of six from the line. Duke pulled off the 85-81 upset. At one point down the stretch, he scored 11 points in 2:20 on five possessions, each time taking the ball to the hoop for the score.

Three decades later Melchionni recalls, "Maryland never adjusted. I can't believe they let me score that many. Maybe they were just stubborn."

After the game some Duke students escaped with the game ball, which they later gave to Melchionni. Although somewhat deflated after 30 years, it still sits on his mantle.

STICKING AROUND

Bucky Waters' attempt to maintain the Duke program was hampered by transfers. Some players left because of academics, some in search of more playing time or a different style of play. Several were publicly critical of Waters, describing an atmosphere of criticism and mistrust. Not everyone felt that way. Gary Melchionni was one key player who remained.

"I never thought about leaving," Melchionni says. "It's not my makeup. You don't deal with those things by running away. We had some prima donnas who thought they were getting yelled at too much. They left for all the wrong reasons. There was definitely some friction there, but I don't have a lot of sympathy for the guys who left."

TIME FOR A CHANGE?

Despite Gary Melchionni's heroics, Duke finished the 1973 season with a five-game losing streak and a 12-14 record. It was Duke's first losing season since 1939, a string surpassed only by Kentucky. Students openly called for Bucky Waters' dismissal, while attendance plummeted and recruiting suffered.

ADOLPH RUPP

Shortly before the start of the 1973-1974 season, embattled Duke coach Bucky Waters asked for a vote of confidence and a contract extension. He was rebuffed and promptly resigned.

Duke athletic director Carl James reached an agreement with former Kentucky coach Adolph Rupp, who had retired in 1972. Rupp was going to coach Duke on an interim basis for one season, while James conducted a thorough search for a permanent coach.

Before the deal could be finalized, Rupp's business partner in Kentucky died. Rupp then declined the job, which went to Duke assistant Neil McGeachy.

"I think it would have worked," James says. "Everybody knew it was only for one year. Rupp brought credibility. But when it became apparent that it wasn't going to work, we moved on."

NEIL McGEACHY

Neil McGeachy's season was not a success. The young assistant was thrown into the deep end of the pool, and he sank. Duke won only 10 times.

The season did contain one highlight, however. On February 13, Duke defeated Virginia 88-78 to become the seventh team in NCAA history to win 1,000 games. Duke won only one more time that season and finished the year with 16 losses, a school record.

GONE, GONE, GONE

The most famous game that season was a heartbreaking Duke loss. A 10-14 Duke team finished its regular season with the short bus trip to Chapel Hill. Despite support from the players, Neil McGeachy clearly was on his way out. Led by Bobby Jones and Walter Davis, North Carolina was ranked fourth in the polls. On paper, it was a total mismatch.

What happened was one of the most unlikely near misses in college basketball history. The inspired Duke team beat the famed UNC press for layup after layup. Point guard Kevin Billerman had 14 assists, and center Bob Fleisher battled Jones for 17 points and 18 rebounds.

Duke led by eight points with just 17 seconds left. After a pair of Duke turnovers, a missed free throw, and four UNC field goals, the last a 35-foot banked shot by Davis at the buzzer, the eight-point lead was gone. UNC won in overtime 95-92.

This tale has become a staple of college basketball broadcasts. Two facets generally are left out. Few remember that despite the shock of Davis' shot, Duke actually led much of the overtime before several key players fouled out. Even more importantly, few realize how well an undermanned Duke team played to put itself in position to pull off a most unlikely upset.

"I felt like I had been punched in the stomach," Tate Armstrong, whose two free throws gave Duke its eight-point lead, says. "To go from the exhilaration of a huge win to the way the game ended was awful."

McGeachy described himself as "devastated," a feeling shared by the entire Duke team. Duke lost its ACC Tournament opener to Maryland, and McGeachy was dismissed shortly afterward.

BILL FOSTER

Carl James hired Bill Foster to replace Neil McGeachy in March 1974. Foster had just taken Utah to the NIT finals. But the Pennsylvania native was an Easterner at heart. He came back every summer to run camps in the Poconos, and he still had relatives in the East.

"I knew Duke from the Bubas years when they were great, and I thought they could be great again, should be great again," Foster says. "I was a little shocked actually when they offered me the job. It just seemed like a great place to coach."

THE COMPETITION

The University of North Carolina is located about eight miles from Duke. UNC is a state-supported school with lots of students, mostly from North Carolina. Duke is a private school, with a smaller enrollment and a student body that is largely from out of state. The combination means that UNC will always have a larger fan base in North Carolina than Duke will.

Bill Foster discovered this fact of life the hard way. When he was at Utah, he had a program entitled "Challenge the Utes" where he and

Bill Foster

a player or two would visit a local school. They would talk, answer questions, and challenge several students in a foul-shooting contest. Foster would end the program by showing the Utah recruiting film.

Foster tried to do the same thing at Duke. Shortly after arriving in Durham, he and some players attended a local school. Foster didn't have a recruiting video yet, so he showed the ACC highlights film.

"This was a big mistake," Foster recalls. "Duke was barely mentioned in the film. UNC comes on the film, and the whole place starts cheering. I was just looking for a place to hide."

UNC and their coach, Dean Smith, would become a perpetual thorn in Foster's side. Foster was fond of saying that before he came to Duke, he had thought Naismith invented basketball, not Dean Smith. After a big Duke win Foster would rhetorically ask reporters how many basketball programs there were in North Carolina.

One time in a pregame meeting in the locker room Foster was angrily berating the media advantage enjoyed by UNC and slammed a piece of chalk against the wall. The chalk bounded back into a chalk holder.

Foster paused for a second and dead-panned to his players, "I bet you don't think I can do that again, do you?"

QUICK WIT?

Bill Foster was one of the most quotable coaches ever. He was wry, self-deprecating, occasionally caustic, but rarely cruel. A typical Foster line came from the middle 1970s. Duke had a player named Willie Hodge who set records for committing personal fouls. After the short bus trip to North Carolina, one of the Duke players was looking for Hodge.

"Where's Willie?" he asked

"He's not playing today," Foster replied. "He fouled out on the way over."

His quick wit hid a fierce competitive desire.

"Foster took those close losses so hard, you were worried about him," Terry Chili says of his coach. "You really wanted to work hard for him."

Foster suffered a series of agonizingly close losses. Once against Wake Forest, Duke scored 109 points and lost. By 13.

"I underestimated how tough the league was," Foster says. "I knew it was tough at the top, but everybody was tough. In order for us to move up, somebody else had to move down. And nobody was looking to move down.

"[After a tough loss,] I would lay awake at night and replay every second. I knew I was on the right track, but sometimes I wondered if I had made a big mistake leaving Utah."

OFF AND RUNNING

Bill Foster immediately decided that Duke would run.

"We had to run to bring back fans and to impress the recruits we needed to recruit to win at this level," he explains. "If we could win some games, all the better."

"Foster really brought back enthusiasm for Duke basketball," says Tate Armstrong, one of the players he inherited. "His style of ball was so much fun to play and to watch. He let us know right away that we would play an up-tempo game, full-speed for 40 minutes."

Duke even produced a bumper sticker with the slogan "Off and Running with the Blue Devils."

TERRY CHILI

Terry Chili was a career reserve. A 6-foot-11 center, Chili was likeable, sometimes goofy. Teammates describe him as "everyone's little brother."

Chili had one moment of glory at Duke. Duke hosted Maryland in February 1976. The Terps were ranked seventh, while Duke was struggling to get to .500. Star freshman Jim Spanarkel sprained his ankle early in the game and didn't return. Willie Hodge fouled out, as he frequently did. Hodge was replaced by Chili, a senior who had barely scored 200 points in his Duke career. Duke led 65-63 with 30 seconds left when Chili went to the foul line. A career 48-percent foul shooter, Chili was not the player Duke wanted on the line.

"Trust me, it was the last place I expected to be," Chili says. "The basket looked about as big as a penny."

But he made three clutch free throws in the dying seconds, and Duke held on for a 69-67 upset.

"The game definitely was the highlight of my career," Chili recalls. "In fact, the last minute of the game was the highlight of my career."

TATE ARMSTRONG

Bill Foster didn't inherit an entirely bare cupboard. Tate Armstrong was a guard from Houston, who had been recruited by Bucky Waters but never played for him. Despite being only 6-foot-2, Armstrong played center for his high school basketball team in Texas. Waters took a chance that Armstrong could make the switch to guard, and it paid off in a big way. Armstrong's high school coach, Roy Kieval, was scorekeeper for the Houston Rockets and helped him get some scrimmage time with the Rocket players. Mike Newlin was so impressed that he praised him to his roommate Jack Marin, who contacted Waters.

Armstrong spent much of his first two seasons on the bench because of assorted injuries and illnesses, including a bout with mononucleosis.

"We thought that if Tate were in better shape, he could reduce his injuries and be a little quicker," Foster explains. "We suggested he take up distance running."

Did he ever. Armstrong went home to Houston and soon was running 20 miles per day in the Texas heat.

"We didn't expect that," Foster says. "Tate willed himself into a great player. I never had a player work harder."

JUST CAN'T WIN

Tate Armstrong had a spectacular junior season in 1976. He shot more than 52 percent from the field, despite the fact that most of his shots were from long range. Armstrong averaged more than 24 points per game. He scored 42 points against Clemson and 40 against North Carolina State.

But Duke lost that game to Clemson 90-89. They lost that game to North Carolina State 96-95. Duke lost 10 games by six or fewer points that season. Armstrong agonized over the series of losses.

"I struggled with the fact that I was scoring so much while we were losing," he says. "Sometimes I felt like I had to shoot every time down the court. It was frustrating. The individual accomplishments were great, but you're judged on how you do as a team."

"We had no problem with Tate shooting as much as he did," Foster confesses. "We knew it was our best chance, maybe our only chance, to beat good teams. We told Tate to keep shooting until his right arm fell off, and then we'd talk about getting him a new arm."

JIM SPANARKEL

Bill Foster was slowly putting together a team. His first significant recruit was 6-foot-5 Jim Spanarkel, a tough New Jerseyite. Spanarkel came to Duke in the fall of 1975 largely because Foster promised him he also could play baseball. Spanarkel pitched and played shortstop at Duke for two seasons before giving up that sport.

Spanarkel wasn't highly recruited. He picked Duke over teams such as Holy Cross and William & Mary.

"I can't say we knew Jim would be as good as he became, but I think we deserve credit for seeing the potential," Foster explains. "We knew we had something special early in practices. No matter how we divided up the teams, the team that Jim was on always seemed to win. He just had a knack for doing the right thing."

Eventually it was said that an opponent that had been beaten by his skill and smarts had been "Spanarkeled."

Spanarkel reveled in his role as team leader. He was team captain as a junior and as a senior.

"I was proud of the captainship because of what it represented," Spanarkel says. "I tried to understand personalities. I tried to set the tone, play aggressively and with a blue-collar mentality. I wanted to have the ball in my hands at the end of the game. I tracked the ball down. I wanted to get to the line, wanted to have the game in my hands."

"He had an unbelievable basketball IQ," teammate Mike Gminski adds. "He had a great sense of what we needed and when we needed it. No question it was his team."

MIKE GMINSKI

It's fair to say that Mike Gminski was the best pure center to ever play at Duke. A precocious student and player, Gminski graduated from high school a year early. Nonetheless, he started his first game at Duke and never came close to losing that starting job.

Former Duke player Terry Chili was a camp counselor in Maryland one summer when Gminski mentioned that he was thinking about graduating early from his Monroe, Connecticut, high school. Chili recognized the camper's potential and clued in Bill Foster and his staff. Gminski visited the Duke campus and, as was the case with so many potential recruits, fell in love with what has been called a Gothic Wonderland.

Despite being only 17 years old, Gminski averaged 15 points and almost 11 rebounds per game as a freshman, outplaying such notables at Clemson's Wayne "Tree" Rollins and Washington's James Edwards.

A COSTLY WIN

For the 1976-1977 campaign Mike Gminski joined holdovers Tate Armstrong, Jim Spanarkel, and Mark Crow, a smooth-shooting six-foot-eight forward. For the first half of the season it looked like Bill Foster's team had turned the corner. Duke upset North Carolina State in the Big Four Tournament, ending a nine-game losing streak against the Wolfpack. Armstrong scored 35 points, including a dramatic buzzer-beater, as Duke edged Washington 83-81. Most impressive was an 81-78 road win over nationally ranked Tennessee and their Bernie and Ernie combo of Bernard King and Ernie Grunfeld.

Duke was 10-1 and was receiving votes for the top 20 for the first time since 1971. But Duke needed to win in the ACC to show they

Mike Gminski

were completely back. More particularly Duke needed to win on the road. Duke entered the 1977 season on the short end of a 27 ACC road-game losing streak, which dated to 1972. Duke went to Virginia determined to end that slide.

"I had never won an ACC road game, and we were determined to win this one," Armstrong recalls.

Early in the game Armstrong went down hard on his right wrist.

"I knew right away I had broken it," he recalls. "The pain was intense."

Trainer Max Crowder tried to look at the wrist during halftime, but Armstrong refused.

"I yelled at Max and actually threw a bucket of ice against the wall at halftime. I was so angry, but we were going to win that game. They were going to have to shoot me to get me off the court."

Armstrong played through regulation and through an overtime. He scored 33 points leading Duke to a hard-fought 82-74 win. It was a costly win. Armstrong's wrist was indeed broken, and his Duke career was over. Minus their leader, Duke lost a succession of tight games and finished 14-13. It was Duke's first winning season since 1972 but was small consolation after the great start.

GENE BANKS

In the midst of this season-ending slump, Bill Foster received what might have been the best news of his Duke career. Foster had spent the autumn of 1976 and the winter recruiting Philadelphia schoolboy sensation Eugene Banks. Duke's competition for Banks was formidable. Notre Dame, UCLA, North Carolina, and Pennsylvania were all on Banks' short list.

One time Foster went to see Banks in a high school game. Other college coaches were there, and after the game they were all over Banks. Foster decided to play it cool. He hardly spoke to Banks, who asked him if something was wrong.

"I told him that I wasn't sure he was good enough to play for us," Foster recalls. "I was taking a big chance. If he had taken it the wrong way, it was over for us. But Gene just laughed. A few weeks later, he committed."

Gene Banks

DUQUESNE?

"I really didn't know much about Duke," Gene Banks says. "The first time they contacted me, I thought it was Duquesne. I was encouraged to visit by my English teacher, Mr. Detwiler, who pushed Duke's academics. I had a great visit. I loved the campus and the academics, but what really sold me was the people, the people in the program, the people outside the program, the whole Duke community. I saw possibilities in the team. I thought I could help them win. People thought I was crazy, but I think it was divine intervention."

Banks brought a swagger to the team.

"I expected to win. I was not sure how, but we were going to win. I never thought about losing. This rubbed off on the other players."

Bill Foster agrees. "Gene's enthusiasm and confidence were contagious. He brought so much energy to the team. We fed off his energy."

Some questioned Banks' ability to succeed academically at Duke. Foster never had any doubts.

"Gene has such a bright, inquisitive mind. We knew he could do the work at Duke."

THE GIFT OF GAB

Gene Banks is the ultimate extrovert, a nonstop talker. He provided a breath of fresh air to a buttoned-down Duke community.

Bill Foster kept an aerosol can in his office, over which he had taped the word *bull**** detector*, and whenever he thought Banks was going too far, he would reach for the can and spray his office.

JOHN HARRELL

Basketball coaches look high and low for quality basketball players. One of Bill Foster's best players just showed up one day. Durham native John Harrell starred at Hillside High School, located only a few miles from the Duke campus. Yet Duke didn't make any contact with him. He attended another Durham school, North Carolina Central University, where his father was on the faculty. Harrell averaged 20 points per game as a freshman there but was unhappy with the coaching situation. He decided to take a chance and transfer to Duke.

The basketball staff found out and helped him gain admittance in time for the beginning of classes. Harrell went on to start for the 1978 Duke team at point guard. Jim Spanarkel calls him "the unsung hero, steady, smooth, and always under control."

KENNY DENNARD

One of Kenny Dennard's nicknames was "Crash." It was a reference to the enthusiasm with which he dove onto the floor or into the crowd in search of a loose ball. Dennard also was called "Dirt." Also "Dog."

Dennard played basketball with a passion and enthusiasm matched by few. Those traits sometimes got him into trouble. Bright and inquisitive, Dennard was an indifferent student, doing only enough work to stay eligible; he completed his Duke degree well after his playing days ended. He loved parties. He did not love curfews. On the court, Dennard fouled out 25 times, a figure that ties him with Willie Hodge for first on the Duke list.

Despite all this, his coaches and teammates loved him. The 6-foot-8, 220-pound Dennard gave his best every practice and every game. The consummate role player, Dennard did anything to help his team win, draw a charge, attack the boards, hound the opposition's top scorer. A native of King, North Carolina, Dennard was one of the few in-state recruits brought in by Duke in the 1970s. He committed to Duke a few months before Gene Banks came on board and started alongside Banks for four years.

YOUTH WILL BE SERVED

College freshmen became eligible for varsity competition in the 1972-1973 season. At that time it was widely thought that only elite freshmen would be able to contribute, because most would be too young. This went double for competitive teams. Only experienced clubs would be able to compete at the highest levels. The 1978 Duke team was the team that demonstrated that talent could defeat experience.

The entire 1978 season was something of a miracle. After six seasons with no more than 14 wins, the 1978 team advanced to the NCAA title game with a starting lineup of one junior, two sophomores, and two freshmen. Of course, these included three of the best players in Duke history, junior Jim Spanarkel, sophomore Mike Gminski, and freshman Gene Banks.

The younger players were backed up by upperclassmen, many of whom had been starters earlier in their careers. That fact could have been a problem, but it wasn't.

"It was difficult to be an upperclassmen backing up a freshman," Gminski observes. "For a lot of these guys, their time never came. But they handled it pretty well. They had to make their impact in practice. They were an asset."

Forward Harold Morrison, who started in 1977 but lost his starting job when Banks and Kenny Dennard arrived, dubbed the Duke reserves the "Not Ready for Prime-Time Players," after television's *Saturday Night Live*.

BEATING THE HEELS

For much of the 1970s Duke was overshadowed by its nearby rival, the University of North Carolina. UNC beat Duke in Chapel Hill, they beat Duke in Greensboro, they beat Duke in Durham. In fact, Duke lost 16 of 17 to North Carolina in the middle 1970s. The only win came in the 1974 Big Four Tournament and thus was a non-conference game. Many of these were agonizing losses by scores such as 72-70, 73-71, 96-92, 77-74, and 89-87.

This record of futility came to a crashing halt on January 14, 1978, when the unranked Devils shocked the second-ranked Heels 92-84. Mike Gminski dominated inside, with 29 points, 10 rebounds, and four blocks, while Jim Spanarkel added 23 points.

Late in the game the noise in Cameron was deafening. Some compared it to the sound of a jet airplane taking off. Gminski said that he thought the whole building was shaking.

"This was the game when we knew we were back," Spanarkel says. "It was the key game of the season, the game when we knew we could not only compete with anybody, but could beat anybody."

"This was a statement game, the one where we sent a message," Banks adds.

The following week Duke was ranked 17th in the AP poll, the first time the school had been ranked since 1971.

WHY DO YOU THINK THEY CALL THEM FREE?

The 1978 Duke team was one of the best foul-shooting teams ever. Duke led the nation, making 79.1 percent of their free shots, a school record that still stands. Jim Spanarkel made 86 percent of his free shots, while Mike Gminski and John Harrell also were more than 80 percent. Duke made 24 of 24 in a 104-88 win over Davidson, half of them by Spanarkel.

"I never understood why people couldn't make foul shots," Spanarkel says. "It's the one thing you can work on by yourself, any time you want to. Nobody guards you, the ball, the rim, the distance, everything stays the same."

FORD'S FAREWELL

Beginning in 1975 the NCAA allowed two teams from the same conference to compete in the NCAA Tournament. The ACC Tournament champion continued to receive the league's automatic bid, but for all practical purposes the team that finished the regular season in first place was guaranteed a spot in the NCAAs. Duke and North Carolina were tied for first place when Duke made the short trip to Chapel Hill for the 1978 finale. Duke probably was a better team than UNC by this point, but they didn't believe it. UNC senior guard Phil Ford, playing in his final home game, poured in 34 points and UNC held on for an 87-83 win. Bill Foster calls this "as good an individual performance as anyone ever played against us."

"We were a better team than UNC at the time, but we weren't sure of it," Jim Spanarkel notes. "We thought we could win at Chapel Hill, but to win in that environment we had to know we would win, had to be absolutely certain. That little bit of doubt held us back."

A SNOWY DAY

Duke entered the 1978 ACC Tournament as the No. 2 seed behind UNC. Should the two teams meet for the title, Duke would be assured of its first NCAA appearance since 1966. Duke had won only a single ACC Tournament game since Vic Bubas retired. Foster was 0-3. Yet Duke did its part with wins over Clemson and Maryland. UNC, however, was upset by Wake Forest. This set up an unexpected predicament for Duke. Should they lose to Wake in the finals, UNC and Wake Forest would take the two NCAA spots, leaving Duke for the NIT.

"At the beginning of the season, that might have been acceptable," Jim Spanarkel says. "But by that point in the season, we thought we had progressed past that. We would have viewed the NIT as a consolation."

It wasn't easy. Wake led 42-37 at the half before Duke's big three took control. Mike Gminski, Gene Banks, and Spanarkel combined for 67 points, and Duke won 85-77. Banks was so excited that he hyperventilated in the locker room. Earlier in his Duke tenure Bill Foster had joked that it would be a snowy day in Greensboro before Duke won the ACC Tournament. It snowed much of that weekend.

"From the outhouse to the penthouse in one year" was how Foster summed up Duke's unlikely rise.

DODGING A BULLET

Duke's trip to the NCAA Tournament was almost a short one. The team was nervous and tentative against Rhode Island in the opener. Mike Gminski, Jim Spanarkel, and Gene Banks combined for 57 points, 25 by Gminski, but the rest of the team scored only six. Rhode Island missed the first end of two one-and-ones in the final 30 seconds and a layup at the buzzer. Duke escaped with a 63-62 win.

THEM'S FIGHTING WORDS

Duke struggled against Ivy-League champion Pennsylvania in the 1978 NCC Eastern Regional semifinals. Penn seemed to have the game wrapped up with an eight-point lead late. Rather than run out the clock, Penn unwisely attacked the basket. Mike Gminski blocked shots on four consecutive possessions.

Gminski was stunned.

"At first I was surprised, then a little insulted. It's like they didn't think I could do it again."

Duke outscored Penn 16-4 down the stretch and won 84-80.

Most losing coaches would bow out gracefully in that situation. Not Pennsylvania's Bob Weinhauer. After the game he predicted that Duke would have no chance against Villanova in the regional final.

"They don't have any quickness," he said. "I don't see any fast break. They fast-break like a herd of thundering elephants. I don't think they'll be able to keep up with Villanova."

"Usually, I don't worry about bulletin-board material," Jim Spanarkel says, "but this was too much. It's like the guy was trying to insult us. We were pretty pumped for the Villanova game."

"We were pretty hot," Kenny Dennard adds. "We win the game, and they're giving us this stuff. We decided to show these guys what a herd of thundering elephants could do."

Duke jumped to a 21-6 lead and cruised to a 90-72 win over Villanova to advance to its first Final Four since 1966.

MEET ME IN ST. LOUIS

Duke advanced to the Final Four, held in St. Louis. Duke met a Notre Dame team that included eight future NBA players. The Fighting Irish were confident.

"All week we were talking about how well they matched up with Kentucky," Kenny Dennard remembers. "Even in the pregame warmups they were talking trash, calling this the preliminary game. We were accustomed to people not taking us seriously, but by this point we thought we had earned some respect."

There was some bad blood between the two programs. Notre Dame didn't acknowledge the National Letter of Intent and had continued recruiting Gene Banks well into the summer, months after he had signed with Duke.

"We knew what was going on and it bothered us," Bill Foster says. "But Gene told us not to worry, and we tried to play it cool."

Duke jumped to a 43-29 halftime lead. Notre Dame came storming back, but Duke held on, making one key free throw after another. Starting guards Jim Spanarkel and John Harrell made all 18 of their foul shots, and Duke won 90-86. Mike Gminski outscored his future NBA rival Bill Laimbeer 29-7.

"We didn't hear too much talking after the game," Dennard says. "They got real quiet."

A DEATH THREAT

Shortly before the title game against Kentucky, St. Louis police received a death threat directed at Gene Banks. Bill Foster was told, but Banks wasn't told until after the game. Despite that fact, Banks knew something was going on.

"I could tell something was up," he remembers. "I could hear people talking. I was concerned but not scared. I grew up in certain situations where I saw people shot, saw people die. I felt safe on the court. It was my stage, my refuge. I wasn't going to let anyone take that away from me."

TOO MUCH "GOOSE"

Duke advanced to the title game against the University of Kentucky. In contrast to the youthful Duke team, Kentucky featured four seniors in its top six players.

Duke won the media war. In press conferences the Duke players were loose, candid, and irreverent. The buttoned-down Kentucky players were tight-lipped.

In the game, however, Duke was unable to stop Kentucky's Jack "Goose" Givens. The senior forward continually found holes in the Duke zone and made 18 of 27 field goals and scored 41 points to lead Kentucky to a 94-88 win.

"I know it looks like we could have found a way to stop him, but he just kept finding the open spots," Gminski says. "On some of the shots we were hanging all over him, and he kept making them. Give him credit."

"I never assumed we would get back to the Final Four," Bill Foster says. "Too many things have to go right, and only one thing has to go wrong. I still remember that game and still wonder what we could have done differently. It still hurts."

GREAT EXPECTATIONS

With everyone returning, Duke was a prohibitive favorite for the 1979 national title. Duke started off 6-0, but then came a disastrous trip to Madison Square Garden shortly before New Year's Day.

Playing in the Holiday Festival, Duke blew big leads against Ohio State and St. John's and came away with two losses. Duke had gone from being the hunter to being the hunted.

"We never recovered from New York," Jim Spanarkel maintains. "It wounded us, and teams could sense we were wounded."

"We got a lot more respect from our opponents," Bill Foster adds. "In one sense, that's what you want, but maybe we weren't ready for it."

Duke plugged along, winning more than they were losing but continuing to struggle with high expectations.

AIR BALL

Duke ended the 1979 regular season with a home game against North Carolina. A win would give Duke a share of the regular-season crown with the Heels.

Duke won the jump ball and scored immediately to take a 2-0 lead. North Carolina crossed midcourt and spread into their Four Corners offense. Duke stayed back in their zone, occasionally coming out to challenge the ball. A few turnovers enabled Duke to score a point here and there. North Carolina attempted only two shots in the first half. The first occurred when center Rich Yonakor inexplicably threw up a long set shot from the baseline. It was completely off the mark.

"Air ball! Air ball!" the student body cried after the flat-out miss.

North Carolina's Dave Colescott tried a midcourt heave at the end of the half. It also struck only air. Two shots, two air balls.

Duke led 7-0 at the half. UNC played the second half straight and lost 47-40.

Afterward Dean Smith explained that he was concerned that the emotions of the crowd would overwhelm his team. Jim Spanarkel still resents the tactic.

"I felt that they hijacked my senior day, upstaged the game," he laments.

THIN BENCH

Bill Foster never liked to use all of his scholarships.

"Having a lot of guys on the end of the bench, not playing, was not a good idea," he explains. "That equates to too many unhappy guys complaining, and things can fall apart from there."

This was a sound philosophy if a team stayed healthy but could cause problems if it did not. Duke's 1979 postseason was torpedoed by personnel losses. Starting guard Bob Bender had an appendectomy just before the ACC Tournament title game, which Duke lost to North Carolina 71-63. Mike Gminski came down with a stomach virus before the NCAA opener against St. John's. Kenny Dennard sprained an ankle in an impromptu late-night pick-up game. Minus two starters and with a third ailing, Duke fell to St. John's 80-78. Jim Spanarkel scored 16 points and became the first Duke player to score 2,000 career points, but it was small consolation.

A LITTLE WARNING NEXT TIME

Duke retired Dick Groat's number 12 in 1952. Dick Groat was a baseball and basketball star, and the number was retired in the spring. Duke didn't retire another basketball number until 1980, when the decision was made to retire Mike Gminski's number 43. Gminski was notified of the decision the day of his final home game.

"I was in a fog for the first 10 minutes of the game," he remembers. "It was too much going on."

Gminski recovered to score 29 points and lead Duke to an overtime win over Clemson. Duke learned its lesson. The school has retired nine numbers since then but never on senior day.

FOSTER'S LAST RUN

Duke got off a great start in 1979-1980, winning its first 12 games and jumping to No. 1 in the national polls. Injuries to Kenny Dennard and Jim Suddath depleted the thin bench, and Duke suffered a four-game losing streak in midseason. The team also was plagued by rumors that Bill Foster was being courted by South Carolina, whose head coach, Frank McGuire, had announced his retirement effective at the end of the season. Foster downplayed the rumors as long as he could before confirming that he would be leaving Duke as the end of the season.

Duke ended the 1980 regular season by losing 96-71 to North Carolina. The loss dropped Duke to .500 in the conference and out of the AP poll for the first time in two seasons. The promising season was headed to an ugly end. Duke needed to win the ACC Tournament to avoid a trip to the NIT.

ONE MORE TITLE

Amazingly, Duke pulled off an unlikely ACC Tournament title. Third-seeded North Carolina State fell in the opener 68-62. Then

Duke thrashed North Carolina 75-61, less than a week after losing to the Heels by 25. A 39-point turnaround in six days.

The title game against Maryland was a tense struggle, with the two teams rarely separated by more than a few points. A Mike Gminski tip-in gave Duke a 73-72 lead late. Maryland's Albert King missed a jumper with just a few seconds left. Maryland center Buck Williams went for the rebound but was undercut by Kenny Dennard. After a tense pause it became clear that the officials had not called a foul, and the game was over.

"I saved Buck from being a goat," Dennard maintains. "I tell him that he would have missed the free throw and all of the Maryland fans would blame him. Now they just blame me."

Williams made 62 percent of his free throws at Maryland, so Dennard may have a point.

Duke also may have been aided by its secret weapon, a massive snowfall in Greensboro.

"If we could only play the ACC Tournament in Alaska every year, we'd have it made," Bill Foster quipped.

REVENGE?

Duke won its NCAA opener over Pennsylvania 52-42. This set up a match against Kentucky on the Wildcats' home court in Lexington. Duke was outraged that they had to play such an important game on a hostile court.

"We used that outrage to our benefit," coach Bill Foster says. "It took our minds off the coaching change and put it back on the court.

Duke jumped all over the Wildcats early, leading 37-23 at intermission, but Duke went cold after halftime. Kentucky tied the game 54-54 before Gene Banks gave Duke a one-point lead with a free throw. Kentucky's Kyle Macy missed a shot at the buzzer, and Duke escaped with a 55-54 win.

"It was a tremendous win, very gratifying," Foster says. "It didn't make up for 1978, but it sure felt good."

PURDUE SENDS DUKE HOME

Duke met Purdue and their All-America center Joe Barry Carroll in the Mideast Regional Finals. Duke jumped to an early lead and still led 30-28 at intermission. However, Duke ran out of gas in the second half, and Purdue pulled away for a 68-60 win.

"We all thought we were better than Purdue and still feel that way," Gene Banks says. "But maybe the pressure had finally gotten to us. We didn't play well."

SOUTH CAROLINA

Why did Bill Foster leave Duke?

"South Carolina did a great job of recruiting me," he says. "They presented a very vivid idea of where they thought I could take them. I guess I was always looking for a chance to rebuild. I probably was a little bit vulnerable when they approached me. Recruiting wasn't going well. I was disappointed in the way the season had gone. I thought we should have had a better year.

"[After the loss to Purdue,] I had some moments when I wondered whether I had done the right thing or not. I looked around the locker room and realized I would never coach Duke again. But I resolved not to look back."

"I think Foster was just more comfortable building a program than sustaining a program," Jim Spanarkel theorizes. "It was just something in his makeup, his personality.

"If I had it to do all over again, I would come to Duke and play for Bill Foster in a heartbeat. He brought so much to the table. He was so likeable and so well prepared. I can't ever remember a time when he annoyed me, a time when I didn't like him, a time when I didn't connect with him."

Foster coached at South Carolina and Northwestern through 1993. He survived a near-fatal heart attack at courtside in South Carolina in 1982.

Chapter 5

THE BEGINNING OF THE COACH K ERA

COACH WHO?

Bill Foster's resignation was effective immediately following the end of the 1980 season. His successor was the source of much conjecture. One local columnist assured his readers that it would be Coach W. It was a logical guess. Foster assistant Bob Wenzel, Old Dominion head coach Paul Webb, and Mississippi head coach Bob Weltlich were the names being bandied about in public.

The surprise announcement that Army's Mike Krzyzewski would be the new Duke coach fulfilled the prediction. Across the state, the announcement was met with the question Coach Who?

The school newspaper, *The Chronicle*, headlined "Krzyzewski: This is Not a Typo." *The Fayetteville Observer* followed with "Duke gets tongue-twister for coach." *The Winston-Salem Journal* called Krzyzewski's selection "a stunning finish to the hunt for a successor to Bill Foster."

BUTTERS' DECISION

Tom Butters was athletic director at Duke for two decades. For many people, that entire tenure can be reduced to one accomplishment. He was the man who hired Mike Krzyzewski.

Butters approached Indiana's Bob Knight about the job. Knight suggested he talk to Krzyzewski, who had played for Knight at Army, assisted Knight at Indiana for one season, and been head coach at

Mike Krzyzewski

Army for five seasons. Knight told Butters that Krzyzewski was "the best young basketball mind in the country."

"He has all of my best qualities and none of my bad ones," he added.

Butters introduced his new coach with the prediction, "I realize Mike's not a household name, but he will be a household name."

NOT THAT GUY

Mike Krzyzewski played for Bob Knight. He was an assistant under Bob Knight. Knight recommended Krzyzewski to Duke. Krzyzewski used Knight's signature motion offense and shared Knight's disdain for zone defenses. Not surprisingly, Krzyzewski spent a considerable amount of time trying to convince people that he wasn't a clone of Knight.

When he introduced to Duke in March 1980, Krzyzewski cautioned, "I think very highly of Coach Knight. But I'm not Bobby Knight. I'm a different person. I admire his principles, but I fit them to my own personality. I think you make a mistake by being somebody else."

THE SECRET

What has made Mike Krzyzewski one of the most successful coaches in college history?

"Coach K can bring in All-Americans and good players and role players and get them on the same page, get them to buy into the system," says Robert Brickey, who played at Duke from 1986 to 1990. "It sounds simple, but it isn't. He has the ability to articulate a vision, to convey his goals in a way that is both passionate and analytical. He wants people who want to work for the common good, to belong to something bigger than themselves, to have a dream."

SPRING BREAK

Kenny Dennard remembers when he first heard that Mike Krzyzewski had become the new coach at Duke.

"I was on spring break in Key West. It wasn't really spring break. True spring break always took place during the season, so I took my own when the season was over. I missed some classes, but I really needed the break. I thought about coming back early but thought some more and stuck around. When I first met Coach K, he gave me that 'where have you been look' but didn't say anything."

JIM SUDDATH

Jim Suddath was a 6-foot-6 forward from Atlanta who came to Duke in the same class as Gene Banks and Kenny Dennard. Suddath was a role player whose career was hampered by injuries. He had surgery shortly after the end of the 1980 season.

"I was on crutches the first time I met Coach Krzyzewski," he remembers. "I didn't see him again until the summer, when I reinjured my knee and had surgery again. He came to see me in the hospital. I didn't see him again until the first day of practice. My knee locked up, and I fell down about five times."

Suddath had more surgery.

"[I woke up] convinced that my basketball career was over," Suddath explains. "The new coach didn't have any kind of investment in me. If I were Coach K, I would have written me off. But he didn't. He gave me a chance."

GOING OUT IN STYLE

Most colleges celebrate senior day, the last home game of the season and thus the last home game of any senior's career. Few Duke seniors have had a more spectacular senior day than Gene Banks did in 1981. Duke's opponent that day was the 11th-ranked North Carolina Tar Heels. Duke went into the game with a 14-11 record. The flashy forward sent the already sky-high crowd into the stratosphere when he distributed roses in the pregame introductions, four in all, one to each corner of the student section.

Still Duke was outmanned. Despite a gritty effort, it looked like Duke would come up short. A pair of Sam Perkins free throws gave UNC a 58-56 lead with only two seconds remaining. Duke had only a single timeout left. It looked hopeless.

UNC called a timeout after the Perkins free throws. This enabled Duke to set up the first pass, a throw to Kenny Dennard near midcourt. Dennard caught the ball and quickly called Duke's last timeout. One second left. Coach Mike Krzyzewski drew up a play in which Banks would act as a decoy, and Dennard would pass to either

Tom Emma or Chip Engelland for the last shot. As Duke was going back on the floor, Banks turned to Dennard.

"Get me the ball!" he told Dennard.

Dennard did just that. A perfect ball fake froze the UNC defenders, and Dennard threw a 50-foot strike to Banks. Banks caught the pass and buried a 20-foot jumper just over the outstretched fingertips of Perkins as the clock hit zero.

Banks scored six points in overtime, including the final two, when he rebounded a Vince Taylor miss with only seconds left. Duke won 66-65. Banks scored 25 of those points.

Following the game, Duke students lifted Banks up and carried around Cameron on their shoulders.

"This is the closest I've ever been to heaven," Banks said after the game.

THE GO-TO GUY

After a first-round loss to Maryland in the ACC Tournament, Duke accepted an invitation to the NIT. Duke hosted North Carolina A&T State in the opener. Duke won comfortably 79-69 but lost Gene Banks early to a broken wrist.

Duke's second game was at home against Alabama. Duke turned to Kenny Dennard.

"It was the only game since I high school that I didn't have to pass the ball," Dennard recalls. "It was fun to be the go-to guy again."

Dennard responded with 23 points and 10 rebounds, and Duke pulled off the upset 75-70. Fellow senior Jim Suddath added 16 points, repaying coach Mike Krzyzewski's faith in him.

Purdue ended Duke's season the next week, however, 81-69.

DUKE BEGINS WITH D

From the very beginning Mike Krzyzewski's trademark was a suffocating man-to-man defense.

In 1981, long before Krzyzewski had any significant success, Clemson coach Bill Foster observed, "The last team in this league I want to play is Duke. They get on you the first second you set foot outside the locker room and don't give you any room to breathe till you get back inside there. It's awful."

VINCE TAYLOR

By 1982 Vince Taylor was the last reminder of Bill Foster's glory days. A 6-foot-5 guard, Taylor had a spectacular season, leading the ACC with more than 20 points per game and leading Duke with five rebounds per game. It wasn't enough to keep Duke afloat. Duke lacked size, depth, and quickness.

The season did have one highlight for Taylor. On February 24 Taylor played his final game in Cameron, against Clemson. Taylor scored a career-high 35 points. The last two came with 27 seconds left in the third overtime and gave Duke a 73-72 lead. Taylor then forced Clemson's best player, Vince Hamilton, into a turnover that sealed the win. Taylor played 51 minutes in the game. The win was Duke's 10th and last of the season, keeping alive the nation's longest streak of consecutive double-digit win seasons. Duke last failed to win at least 10 games in 1928.

After the game Taylor told the crowd, "I'm gonna call Gene and tell him I outdid him. For the first time, I outdid him."

Gene, of course, was Gene Banks, who had had a memorable senior day the previous season.

DAN MEAGHER

Dan Meagher was one of three Canadians who have played basketball at Duke. A six-foot-seven forward, he was one of Mike Krzyzewski's first recruits at Duke. He also was one of the most physical players ever to wear an ACC uniform. He was the master of the subtle elbow to the ribs, the casual stepping on toes. His specialty was to grab an opposing player's waistband and pull him down over him, inducing a charging call.

Meagher had some legendary battles with Virginia bruiser Tom Sheehey. At one time the ACC introduced players one at a time, alternating teams. The opposing players met at midcourt and politely shook hands. In 1985 Meagher slapped Sheehey's hand with such force that Duke radio announcer Bob Harris "thought that he was going to knock Sheehey's arm out of his socket." Shortly afterward, the ACC decided to dispense with the midcourt handshake. It was not a coincidence.

Later that game, according to Meagher, Sheehey said something about Meagher's mother that the Duke forward didn't appreciate, so he spat in Sheehy's face. On his subsequent visits to Cameron, Sheehey was met with "Meagher spit on you" chants from the Duke students.

"Meagher was from Canada, and he had that hockey player's mentality," Harris recalls. "If he wanted to get the ball, he would get the ball. If someone was in his way, too bad. He would go through a wall for a loose ball."

Meagher agrees.

"I played hockey for 12 years. I was a physical hockey player, so you can imagine how that translated to the basketball court. I knew I wasn't going to outjump anyone or outquick anyone, so I had to outwork them. I was physical, but I don't think I was dirty. I never tried to hurt anyone."

BEG YOUR PARDON?

On December 5, 1981, Duke suffered an embarrassing home loss to Appalachian State University.

The next morning the telephone rang at the Jay Bilas home. Bilas was a high school star in Rolling Hills, California, who was being recruited by Duke. His mother answered the phone. An assistant coach at one of the other schools recruiting Bilas was on the other end.

"Mrs. Bilas, have you ever heard of Appalachian State?" he asked.

Mrs. Bilas responded that she had not.

"Well, they beat Duke last night," was the response.

Bilas still ended up at Duke.

JOHNNY DAWKINS

Johnny Dawkins was the recruit who turned around Mike Krzyzewski's program. A mercurial 6-foot-2 guard from Washington, D.C. Dawkins turned down Notre Dame, Maryland, and other powerhouse schools for the chance to help revive the Duke program. He was the first of the more than 30 McDonald's All-Americans brought to Duke by Krzyzewski. Dawkins would start all 133 games in his four seasons at Duke and score a school-record 2,556 points, a recorded broken by J.J. Redick in 2006.

Jay Bilas watches as Johnny Dawkins dunks over an Irish defender.

Dawkins was a rare blend of athleticism, intelligence, and skill. He had the ability to get open against any defender. Dawkins once described his offensive moves.

"I'm not sure how I do it. I just look at my defender's feet. You make him react, and you go the other way. It's instinct."

"[He is] the most creative scorer I ever saw in college, the quickest, most deceptive player," Mark Alarie lauds.

DEAR ALMA MATER

Shortly after Johnny Dawkins committed to Duke, he played in the Capital Classic all-star game in D.C. Maryland coach Lefty Driesell, making one last desperate attempt to sway Dawkins, approached him before the game and asked Dawkins why he wanted to go to Duke.

"Why Coach, I admire you so much, and Duke is your alma mater," Dawkins responded.

MARK ALARIE

Mark Alarie signed with Duke just weeks after Johnny Dawkins. Duke's first ever recruit from Arizona, Alarie also started every game at Duke for four years.

"I fell in love with the Duke team of Gminski and Spanarkel and Banks," says Alarie, despite growing up 2,000 miles from Durham. "I was a big fan."

Alarie started his career as a low-post scorer but developed a deadly outside shot. He could play center, power forward, or small forward with equal effectiveness. Less flashy than teammates such as Dawkins, Alarie was an underrated player, who ended his career with 2,136 points.

PLAYING DIRTY?

Johnny Dawkins, Mark Alarie, and Jay Bilas were joined by forwards David Henderson, Bill Jackman, and Weldon Williams in what was regarded as the nation's top recruiting class. Yet the class of 1986 had a rough start. They lost a school-record 17 games in 1983. The season ended with a 109-66 loss to Virginia in the first round of the ACC Tournament, still the biggest margin of defeat in school history. Following the game Virginia's star center Ralph Sampson accused Duke of playing dirty.

"We weren't dirty; we simply weren't good enough to guard him," Bilas says. "But to call us dirty after beating us like they did, well, we didn't forget it."

The Duke coaches and support staff got together after the game at a local restaurant. Sports information director Johnny Moore made a toast.

"Here's to forgetting tonight."

Krzyzewski's response: "Here's to never forgetting tonight."

The coaches weren't the only ones who felt that way. The freshman class vowed to never again lose to Virginia.

"Every weight I lifted, every shot I took, I thought about that game, about getting better, about making sure it never happened again," Henderson says.

Duke didn't lose again to Virginia until 1990, a streak of 16 games.

LEARNING D

An aggressive man-to-man defense is the cornerstone of Mike Krzyzewski's program. The freshman-laden team of 1983 wasn't prepared to play that type of defense, but Krzyzewski refused to allow this young team to play zone. Duke permitted almost 84 points per game and gave up 100 or more points seven times. The low point came when Duke lost 84-77 to Wagner College. At home.

"Playing four freshmen in 1983 was a recipe for disaster," Mark Alarie says. "But we were determined to do it the right way, to lay a foundation. We had to be thrown into the fire sooner or later. It might as well have been sooner. There was no substitute for game experience. The freshmen never questioned the strategy behind playing an aggressive man-to-man defense. We knew it would be the ticket to our success."

VIVA LA FRANCE

The Duke team toured France in the summer of 1983. It was a thin squad. The departing seniors weren't allowed to go, nor were the incoming freshmen. Dan Meagher was playing for the Canadian national team.

"The trip brought us together," Mark Alarie says. "Our state of mind wasn't good after the 1983 season. The trip gave us a chance to play some winning basketball. When everybody in the place is against you—the other team, the fans, the referees, the scorekeeper, the ball boys, everyone—you have to pull together. We left our freshman year behind."

ARNOLD

Jay Bilas came to Duke as a forward. He and fellow freshman Mark Alarie, both about six foot eight and 220 pounds, were forced into playing center against much larger opponents.

"We felt like we were boys going against men," Alarie says. "We needed to get much stronger."

Bilas practically lived in the Duke weight room in the off-season, putting on 25 pounds of solid muscle.

"You couldn't believe how his body responded to weightlifting," Alarie recalls. "He had muscles on top of his muscles."

His impressed teammates took to calling him Arnold, after Schwarzenegger. Bilas sacrificed much of his natural mobility in order to fill a need. He spent the rest of his Duke career playing center, regularly guarding players three, four, or five inches taller than him.

"It was no big deal," Bilas explains. "I needed to get bigger, so I got bigger."

MR. CLUTCH

Many recruiting experts considered David Henderson to be an afterthought in the class that was led by Johnny Dawkins, Mark Alarie, and Jay Bilas. A native of rural Warren County, North Carolina, Henderson was "country strong," both physically and mentally.

Henderson developed a reputation for clutch play. He won numerous games in the last seconds, some with field goals, some with free throws, and some with great defense. In 1984 Henderson beat Georgia Tech in Atlanta on a free throw with no time on the clock and a sell-out crowd howling for his head.

"When I was a kid and playing basketball by myself, I always envisioned myself with the ball at the end of a close game," he recalls. "I always took the last shot, and I always made it. Sometimes I was playing for Duke, sometimes for North Carolina State, sometimes for North Carolina, but the outcome was always the same. When I got to Duke and was in clutch situations, it just seemed like it had been in my imagination. I loved being in that position."

"[He was] the toughest player, mentally and physically, I ever played with," Alarie lauds. "He was a vocal, fiery leader, the guy who told us what we needed to hear, even if we didn't want to hear it."

CAMERON CRAZIES

Duke students have unusually close proximity to the court. More than almost any fans in sport, they view themselves as not just spectators but participants. They have gained a national reputation for passion and innovation that occasionally crosses the line. Maryland coach Lefty Driesell, a Duke alum, was a fan favorite. Students would wear skullcaps to mimic his baldness. North Carolina State's Norm Sloan and his players were mocked so relentlessly that Sloan was moved to write a letter to Duke president Terry Sanford predicting "an ugly scene that will provoke national attention."

Sloan was correct. In 1984 Maryland forward Herman Veal was accused of sexual assault. When Veal was introduced at Cameron at the January 14 game, the floor was littered with condoms and women's underwear. Sanford had seen enough. He issued what has become known as the "Uncle Terry letter," in the school newspaper. In it, Sanford, a former North Carolina governor, called on Duke students to be creative not vulgar in support of their team. The request had an immediate effect. The students began responding to a controversial call with chants of "We beg to differ." Opponents were greeted with "Hi" when they were introduced. Signs were posted that read "Welcome esteemed opponents."

DOUBLE STANDARD?

The first game at Cameron after the Uncle Terry letter was the Duke–North Carolina game. Duke was leading 67-64 late in the second half when the game exploded. North Carolina coach Dean Smith had sent a substitute to the scorer's table to go in when the next opportunity arose. The game resumed without the scorekeeper blowing the horn to signal the referees. An angry Smith banged the scorer's table, trying to set off the horn and stop play. He hit the wrong button, inadvertently giving UNC 20 points. The officials sent Smith back to the bench but declined to give him a technical foul.

After the game, in which UNC came back to win 78-73, coach Mike Krzyzewski blasted the officiating.

"I want to tell you something," he said. "When you come in here and start talking about how Duke has no class, you'd better start getting your stories straight—because our students had class and our team had class. There was not a person on our bench who was pointing a finger at the officials or banging on a scorer's table. You cannot allow people to go around pointing at officials and yelling at them without technicals being called. That is just not allowed. So, let's get some things straight around here and quit the double standard that exists in this league, all right?"

Athletic director Tom Butters has always maintained that it was a coincidence, but three days later Duke extended Krzyzewski's contract by five years. Regardless, the young Duke coach clearly had thrown down the gauntlet.

BRICK

Duke had a great chance to end the 1984 regular season by beating UNC in Chapel Hill. Duke led by two points with seven seconds left when Dan Meagher went to the foul line with a chance to wrap up the game.

He missed the free throw.

UNC scored at the buzzer and ended up winning in double overtime.

It is standard for each of the players to have a box in the basketball office where they can pick up mail, autograph requests, and similar items. The Monday after the game, Meagher went to the office and found that assistant coach Tom Rogers had placed a brick in his box, in commemoration of his missed free throw.

"It was done in good humor," Meagher says, "but it also was a motivator."

GETTING EVEN

As has happened numerous times, Duke had a chance to avenge the bitter loss less than a week later, in the ACC Tournament. Going into the tournament with a 7-7 conference mark, Duke had sewn up a likely NCAA bid with an overtime win over Georgia Tech in the first round. Led by Michael Jordan and Sam Perkins, North Carolina was ranked number one in the country and had just completed a 14-0 ACC regular season.

Duke jumped on top early and held on for a riveting 77-75 win. Mark Alarie made nine of 13 shots on the way to a 21-point outing, Jay Bilas held Sam Perkins to nine points, while Johnny Dawkins added 16 points and seven assists. David Henderson made Jordan work for each of his 22 points.

"We had played them tough two times during the season, and before that game we just knew we were going to win," Bilas remembers. "And we knew they were worried about us. We weren't going to surprise them."

Alarie remembers this as a redemptive moment.

"My freshman year we couldn't hang with UNC at all. Then we played them close but couldn't win. Then we got the win. This was a watershed. There was no more questioning ourselves. After that we respected North Carolina, but we never again feared them. We knew we could beat anybody."

GOODBYE TO CARMICHAEL

Duke plays North Carolina in Chapel Hill once every season. Duke won in 1966, the first year that UNC played at Carmichael Auditorium. Duke then proceeded to lose at Carmichael 18 consecutive seasons, some in the most heart-breaking fashion imaginable. The Dean Smith Arena was under construction when Duke made one last trip to Carmichael in 1985.

Duke had won its first 12 games that season to jump to No. 2 in the polls, trailing only Patrick Ewing and Georgetown. However, Duke came into Chapel Hill after having lost to Maryland in overtime and Wake Forest in double overtime.

Duke used its quickness to overcome UNC's size advantage.

"Given UNC's size, we weren't going to get a lot inside off our halfcourt offense," Mark Alarie says. "But we knew our big guys could beat their big guys down the court and get good shots."

This was exactly what happened. Guards Johnny Dawkins and Tommy Amaker broke the press, Alarie and Jay Bilas scored 19 and 17 points respectively. But the game belonged to Dawkins, who scored 34 points and pulled down eight rebounds. Duke broke open a close game in the middle of the second half to win 93-77.

The win was huge for senior forward Dan Meagher, who had a contentious relationship with UNC coach Dean Smith, who considered him a dirty player.

"Beating Dean at his place was very gratifying," Meagher says. "But more importantly this game juxtaposed where we had been and how far we had come. I remember playing them early in my career when guys like James Worthy and Sam Perkins pushed us around like we weren't there, like we were boys. Now we were men. We could compete with anybody."

SLAPPING THE FLOOR

It only happens in close games, and it only happens when Duke is on defense. A Duke player, maybe two, perhaps all five, will bend down, slap the floor with both hands, and come back up with fire in the eyes. Mike Krzyzewski would use this technique in practice to illustrate a point.

"It was K's way of showing us that if we did what he said," Mark Alarie says, "we would own the defensive floor, that no one would get by around us."

Gradually the team adopted this as a motivational tool on big defensive possessions. Sometimes the team would look over to the bench and see Krzyzewski giving the sign, but more often than not a player would initiate the routine.

"It was our way of reminding ourselves of where we were, of how we were in the game," Alarie adds. "We only did it for big plays and tried to not overdo it. We only did it when we were dead serious."

SHUT UP ALREADY

Sometimes the Cameron Crazies outsmart themselves. In 1985 North Carolina State's 6-foot-7, 250-pound forward Lorenzo Charles was involved in some controversy involving paying for a pizza delivery. When he was introduced at Duke, the floor was littered with pizza boxes.

"Right away I was thinking that might not have been a good idea," Mark Alarie says. "Charles was a gentle giant, very mild-mannered.

You always wondered what would happen if somebody made him mad. We found out."

Charles was unstoppable that night, muscling inside for 25 points in leading State to a 70-66 upset win.

THE CLASS OF 1986

Johnny Dawkins, Mark Alarie, David Henderson, and Jay Bilas started their Duke career in the ACC basement, losing a then-school-record 17 games. They ended it by winning an NCAA-record 37 games. They became the first class in NCAA history to have four players score more than 1,000 points. Dawkins ended his career with 2,556 points, only 31 points shy of the ACC record set by Wake Forest's Dickie Hemric in the 1950s, while Alarie totaled 2,136.

THE DEAN DOME

Duke won the first preseason NIT in the fall of 1985, defeating Kansas and St. John's in the final two games. Duke won its first 16 games that season. Game 17 was at Chapel Hill, in the first game played at the Dean E. Smith Center, more widely known as the Dean Dome. North Carolina was also undefeated and was ranked No. 1; Duke was No. 3. Mark Alarie scored the first basket in the Dean Dome.

"It wasn't that big a deal then or now," he explains. "We were more concerned with the game. I guess I'm the answer to a trivia question, but I would rather have won the game."

North Carolina broke open the close game in the middle of the second half and jumped to a 16-point lead in the second half. A furious Duke rally fell short, and UNC won 95-92. Duke lost its next game 87-80 at fourth-ranked Georgia Tech. Duke would not lose again for a long time.

BUSY WEEKEND

Mike Krzyzewski likes to tweak Duke's schedule based on his perception of his team's strengths and weaknesses. Less talented or less experienced teams are more likely to get confidence builders, while more talented teams receive more challenges. Krzyzewski knew that his 1986 squad was loaded, so he scheduled accordingly. Duke won the Big Apple NIT in New York and played a difficult non-conference schedule. In mid-February Duke scheduled a Sunday afternoon home game against potent Notre Dame. Nothing surprising about that—except that Duke was already scheduled to play at North Carolina State on Saturday night. Two regular-season games in two days, both against teams ranked in the top 20. This was virtually unheard of.

Duke passed the test. Barely. Duke fell behind North Carolina State 17-6 but caught up with the Wolfpack shortly after intermission. The second half featured nine lead changes and 11 ties, the last 70-70. Duke had the ball for the last shot, but Johnny Dawkins was trapped on the baseline, 23-feet from the basket. His desperation shot missed everything, but State's Nate McMillan was whistled for a foul.

"I never touched him," McMillan said after the game, "I just held my hands up in the air, but he did a great selling job."

Dawkins told a different story.

"He bumped me across the arm. Besides, I'm a basketball player not an actor."

Dawkins' two free throws gave Duke the 72-70 win.

Duke's game against Notre Dame was equally tense. Duke led 75-69 with less than a minute left but committed a turnover and missed the first end of two one-and-ones. Trailing 75-74, Notre Dame had the ball and a chance to win. Defensive stopper Tommy Amaker had fouled out, leaving Dawkins with the job of defending Notre Dame star David Rivers. As expected, Rivers took the last shot. Or tried to. Dawkins stuffed it, preserving Duke's second nail-biting win in less than 24 hours. Rivers complained that there had been some contact on the play.

Dawkins responded, "Yes, my hand on the ball. That's contact."

GOING OUT IN STYLE

It's tempting to think of big-time college basketball players as impervious to pressure. Not so. On March 2, 1986, Duke seniors Mark Alarie, Johnny Dawkins, David Henderson, Jay Bilas, and Weldon Williams played their final home game. The opponent was North Carolina, and first place in the ACC was at stake.

"I had trouble sleeping last night," Alarie said after the game. "Physically I didn't feel that well today. I had butterflies in my stomach. I had no appetite. I felt very different from any other game

I've ever played in. I never felt the pressure of one game as much as this one. It was as important to us as any game we played in four years. We were worried, if we did lose, it would spoil a very successful season."

Keep in mind this was a star senior playing in his 124th college game.

Duke won the game 82-74. Seniors Henderson, Dawkins, and Alarie overcame the butterflies for 27, 21, and 16 points respectively. The win gave Duke its first undisputed first-place finish in the ACC since 1966.

THE FIRST ONE

Duke went into the 1986 ACC Tournament as the top seed and the nation's No. 1 seed. Close wins over Wake Forest and Virginia put Duke into the finals, against Georgia Tech. Led by All-America guard Mark Price, the sixth-ranked Yellow Jackets provided fierce competition. Duke led by as many as nine points in the second half, but Tech fought back to take the lead. The teams traded baskets down the stretch until a Mark Alarie jumper gave Duke a 66-65 lead with 45 seconds left.

"We knew they would put the ball in Price's hands," Alarie says. "Who wouldn't? We were determined to take it back out of his hands and make somebody else beat us."

Duke's defense suffocated Price, forcing him to pass to teammate Craig Neal, whose hurried 18-footer was off the mark. Johnny Dawkins grabbed the rebound and made a pair of foul shots. Tech countered with a basket too late to change the outcome.

This marked the first time Duke had finished first in the regular season and won the tournament since 1966.

I CAN'T JUMP THAT FAR

Duke was staying in a Greensboro hotel when the fire alarm went off about 5 a.m. the morning of Duke's semifinal game against Virginia. David Henderson was the first player out of the building, running down all 14 flights of stairs.

"I wasn't taking any chances," Henderson says. "I can't jump that far, but I sure can run that far."

Henderson wasn't sleeping that well, anyway. He told reporters that roommate Johnny Dawkins had talked in his sleep all night about being the tournament MVP.

Dawkins's dreams were right on the mark. He was named ACC Tournament Most Outstanding Player.

A BIG SCARE

Duke entered the 1986 NCAA Tournament ranked No. 1 in the country. They opened in Greensboro, only 50 miles away, against an unheralded Mississippi Valley State team. Naturally, Duke almost lost. Playing at noon on a Thursday, Duke was flat and disinterested. Mississippi Valley State's quickness and aggressive zone defense put Duke back on its heels. Tommy Amaker compared them to "a bunch of tigers." Duke trailed 40-37 at halftime and fell behind by seven before rallying. Johnny Dawkins led Duke back with 27 points—16 in one five-minute stretch—and Duke survived 85-78.

After the game Dawkins told coach Mike Krzyzewski that one day he would ask him for a coaching job, and if Coach K gave him a hard time, he would mention that game.

It was Duke's toughest game in the Eastern Regional. Old Dominion, DePaul, and Navy fell, sending Duke to its first Final Four since 1978.

K'S FIRST FINAL FOUR

Duke's first opponent was Kansas, a team Duke had edged earlier in the season in New York. Duke was ranked No. 1 in the country; Kansas No. 2. Kansas was a physical team, led by 260-pound center Greg Dreiling and powerful wing Ron Kellogg, who led Kansas with 22 points. Kansas led 65-61 with two minutes left, but Duke's stifling defense shut down the Jayhawks down the stretch, and Duke won 71-67. Johnny Dawkins led all scorers with 24 points, but the true hero may have been Mark Alarie, whose suffocating defense held Kansas' star Danny Manning to four points.

The brutal game was draining. Duke's final opponent was Louisville, which had cruised to a semifinal win over LSU. Duke led almost the entire way against Louisville. Dawkins scored 18 points in the first half, prompting Louisville coach Denny Crum to switch to a diamond-and-one defense designed to deny Dawkins the ball. Duke forwards Alarie and David Henderson had open shots but missed them.

"After 40 games, our legs were shot," Alarie says. "We kept coming up short on shots because we didn't have any lift."

Alarie and Henderson made only nine of 26 field goals.

Louisville also dominated the boards, outrebounding Duke 38-23. A big offensive rebound and basket by Louisville's Pervis Ellison in the last minute gave the Cardinals a lead they never relinquished in a 72-69 win.

"It never occurred to us that we weren't going to win the national title," Alarie confesses. "We had come so far and came so close."

Years later coach Mike Krzyzewski noted, "If I had known then what I know now, I could have helped my team. But we were weary; we had no legs."

TOMMY AMAKER

Tommy Amaker was a guard from northern Virginia. He came to Duke a year after the Johnny Dawkins-Mark Alarie-David Henderson class and was a four-year starter. Amaker was a classic point guard, concentrating on distributing the ball and playing defense. His defense was stifling.

"Amaker made the biggest difference defensively," Alarie explains. "He could apply so much pressure on the other team's point guard that he prevented teams from running their offense. Sometimes I almost felt sorry for the other team's point guards. Almost."

Coach Mike Krzyzewski has said that Amaker was "the best person I ever coached."

"We always joked that Coach K had adopted Tommy," Alarie says. "We would ask Tommy what Dad had planned for the next practice."

Robert Brickey was a freshman when Amaker was a senior.

"Tommy was so thorough and so professional. He was always on time, always had his classes in order, was always prepared. Little stuff, but the little stuff wins championships, and he taught us that."

PIZZA ANYONE?

Tommy Amaker's freshman roommate was Marty Nessley, Duke's other recruit in the high school class of 1987. A bigger contrast could scarcely be imagined. Amaker was a 6-foot-1, 160-pound African-

American from the D.C. suburbs. Nessley was a 7-foot-2, 280-pound Caucasian from a small town in Ohio. The meticulous Amaker would retire at 10 p.m., maybe 11 p.m. on a weekend. Nessley was more interested in examining college life.

Nessley constantly battled his weight. Duke put him on a strict diet.

"Marty would come to the training table and barely eat a thing, a salad maybe," teammate Mark Alarie recalls. "But he couldn't drop any weight. Nobody knew why. Then one night Amaker was asleep at about 1 a.m. or 2 a.m. and he heard a knock at the door. Nessley got up, answered the door, and there was some murmuring. Amaker tried to go back to sleep but heard some rustling coming from Nessley's side of the room. He turned on a light and saw that Nessley was eating a pizza under the covers. He had been doing that all season. Mystery solved."

TOO SMALL?

College athletes can be great practical jokers.

"You can tell who the gullible guys are right away," Mark Alarie muses. "Quin Snyder would believe anything. One day Jay [Bilas] and I were telling him how small the Duke lockers were, how you could actually step into a locker at the other ACC schools. Quin insisted that he could step into a Duke locker."

After some cajoling, Snyder proved his point. Alarie and Bilas locked the door behind him and pretended to leave, ignoring Snyder's increasingly frantic calls for several minutes.

"You had to be able to take stuff like that if you were going to survive a long season," Alarie adds. "The thin-skinned just weren't going to make it."

A PROGRAM NOT A TEAM

Duke started four seniors in 1986, three of whom played in the NBA the following season. Absent these stars, Duke started the 1987 season unranked and picked to finish sixth in the ACC. But Mike Krzyzewski disagreed.

"No team with Tommy Amaker on it can be said to be rebuilding. He won't allow it. I don't see us going 11-17 again. Put it this way. We better not go 11-17 again."

He was right. Duke went 24-9, finished third in the ACC, and advanced to the third round of the NCAA Tournament.

"There's a difference between developing a good team and developing a good program that can be sustained over a period of time," says sophomore Danny Ferry, who developed into an All-ACC player that season. "We all knew what people were saying about us before the season and used it as motivation. We proved that Duke was a program not a flash in the pan."

Robert Brickey was a freshman in 1987.

"At first I thought we might struggle. Then I listened to Coach K, to his passion and his commitment. I knew that he wasn't looking to take a season off to rebuild, that he simply wouldn't allow it."

TOO MUCH CELEBRATION

There are lots of ways for basketball players to get injured. In 1988 John Smith may have discovered a new one. Duke was playing Rhode Island in the third round of the NCAA Tournament. Smith, a junior forward, drew a key charge on Rhode Island. He was knocked on the floor, near the basket support. The exuberant Smith celebrated by slamming his right hand into the support. He discovered that the padding on the support only went so deep. Smith broke his right hand and missed Duke's next game, the Eastern Regional title game against Temple.

BILLY KING

Mike Krzyzewski's successful tenure at Duke has been built on a bedrock of defensive excellence. Billy King may have been the best defensive player in that period. Standing 6-foot-6 and weighing 205 pounds, he was strong, quick, intelligent, and relentless. King possessed all of the attributes necessary for a defensive stopper. He once hounded Notre Dame All-American David Rivers into a three-of-17 shooting performance.

King saved his best for last. In late March 1988, King's senior season, Duke met Temple for the Eastern Regional championship. The top-ranked Owls went into the game with a 32-1 record. Their key scorer was 6-foot-4 freshman Mark Macon, whose 24 points per game had helped make him an All-American. King only had one day to prepare for Macon, and he spent the day looking at films.

"Obviously I was impressed, but I saw some tendencies I thought I could exploit," King explains. "Macon always wanted to shoot off the dribble, and he preferred to go to his left. I looked at it as a challenge. I thought I was ready."

Was he ever. Macon could scarcely take a breath without King in his face.

"My goal was to make him uncomfortable, to make him go places he didn't want to go," King says. "We wanted to keep him from putting the ball on the floor, just make him uncomfortable."

Macon shot five air balls in just the first half. Macon kept shooting in the second half and kept missing. He ended up six of 29, with seven air balls. Duke upset Temple 63-53 to advance to Mike Krzyzewski's second Final Four.

Kansas ended Duke's season in the first game of the Final Four. Duke fell behind 16-2 and 24-6, rallied to within three points, but fell short 66-59.

NEXT PLAY

"Next play" is one of Mike Krzyzewski's most-oft quoted phrases. Learn what you can, don't look back, move on.

Kevin Strickland elaborates.

"Coach K is the best in the business at playing a game and switching the focus to the next game. Don't get too up following a win or too down following a loss. It's easy to say that but hard to do it. He just has an uncanny ability to focus on what comes next and an innate ability to transfer that focus."

Early in his Duke tenure Krzyzewski said, "We try to get across an attitude where you react fairly much on the same level no matter whether you win or lose."

DANNY FERRY

Danny Ferry was the nation's top recruit in 1985. He selected Duke over North Carolina, the first player to choose Mike Krzyzewski over Dean Smith. Ferry's father, Bob, played 10 seasons in the NBA and later was a longtime NBA general manager.

"Ferry had all the attributes of the classic coach's son," Krzyzewski says. "He was smart, fundamentally sound, understood the game. But

Danny Ferry

most coaches' sons are 6-foot one-1. Danny was 6-foot-10, which made him all the more unique."

Teammate Robert Brickey agrees.

"Danny had an NBA mentality. He knew all the tricks, footwork, ball fakes, that sort of thing. But he also knew how to apply a subtle hip check or forearm that would be effective but wouldn't be obvious."

Ferry would score 2,155 points at Duke, and he and J.J. Redick are the only Duke players to be named ACC Player of the Year after two consecutive seasons.

SUPERHERO

On December 5, 1974, North Carolina State's peerless David Thompson set an ACC record with 57 points. Thompson accomplished this feat before college basketball had either a three-point shot or a shot clock. Yet, as impressive as 57 points is, Thompson did score them in a 144-88 win over an outmatched Buffalo State team. North Carolina State didn't really need Thompson to score that much in order to win the game.

This was not the case when Danny Ferry broke Thompson's record on December 10, 1988. Duke was visiting Miami, and a sellout crowd was on hand to root on the home team. The Hurricanes were small but quick. They hoped an up-tempo game would maximize their chances of pulling off the upset. But they couldn't stop Ferry.

"I was totally in a zone," he recalls. "My mind was so clear and focused. See ball, catch ball, shoot ball."

Ferry had 34 points at intermission. His previous high at Duke was 33. Duke needed all of them. They led only 60-51 at the half.

Ferry broke Dick Groat's school record of 48 with nine minutes left. Duke led 93-74 at that point, but Miami rallied and cut the lead to eight before Duke stabilized and held on for a 117-102 win. Ferry broke the record with the final of two free throws with 44 seconds left. He ended with 58 points on 23 of 26 shooting from the field and 10 of 12 from the foul line. He made only two three-pointers.

"I think Danny was a member of the Hall of Justice tonight," teammate Quin Snyder exclaimed after the game. "Something divine was going on. Danny could have swallowed kryptonite tonight."

Snyder did note that the rest of the Duke team outscored Ferry 59-58.

"It was a freakish game," Ferry says. "Things like that just don't happen. I played in thousands of basketball games. I don't remember the details of most of them, but I remember this one. It was special."

CHRISTIAN LAETTNER

Christian Laettner probably had the best college career of any player in Duke history. A prodigious worker, the 6-foot-11 Laettner put on 30 pounds of muscle at Duke and developed an effective perimeter game. Yet he was a controversial player. He could be abrasive and confrontational. Opposing fans loved to hate Laettner, and he thrived on their disdain.

Teammate Marty Clark says Laettner is misunderstood.

"We always knew he was a leader. He had so many different relationships within the team. He knew who needed to be prodded, who needed to be challenged, who needed to be left alone. He had great instincts."

"Christian was the ultimate perfectionist," Bob Harris says. "He wanted to win at everything. If you didn't subscribe to that view, he could be tough on you. He would see how far he could push you. He would push until you drew a line and said, 'No further.' Then he would respect you. If you didn't draw the line, you wouldn't gain his respect."

Laettner had tremendous confidence.

"What's beyond arrogance?" teammate Brian Davis asked. "That's where Christian is."

"Christian was the most competitive person I ever knew," Greg Koubek says. "Basketball, ping-pong, dating women, whatever it was, he was going to be the best."

Mike Krzyzewski has said Laettner had "fire in his eyes and a passion in every game."

TRIVIA ANSWER

Greg Koubek was the consummate role player for Duke. A 6-foot-6 forward, Koubek played in 147 games for Duke, averaging five points per game. Koubek was a reserve for Duke's 1988, 1989, and 1990 Final Four teams and started for the 1991 NCAA champions. Koubek thus became the first player in NCAA history to play in four

Christian Laettner

Final Fours. Teammates Christian Laettner and Brian Davis accomplished the feat the following year. No one else has done so.

"I've been a gold mine to my friends," Koubek says. "They know the answer, but nobody else does. They've won lots of trivia contests that way."

Koubek's roommate and classmate Clay Buckley was a member of the same four Final Four teams but only played in three of the four. His father, Jay, was a starter on Duke's 1963 and 1964 Final Four teams, while Uncle Bruce played for North Carolina 1977 Final Four team.

NEED A HUG?

Late in the 1989 season Duke played Arizona at Madison Square Garden. Christian Laettner had a chance to tie the game with one second left but missed a foul shot. At the game's conclusion Mike Krzyzewski went to the court and quietly consoled Laettner, telling him that he would make the big shot the next time he had the chance. A few weeks later, Laettner outplayed fellow freshman Alonzo Mourning of Georgetown and led Duke to the Eastern Regional Championship.

Laettner was also consoled by former president Richard Nixon, a Duke Law School graduate, who had attended the game.

"Everything will be fine," Nixon told Laettner. "I know. I've won a few and lost a few myself."

1990

Most people remember the 1990 Duke season only for the way it ended, a 103-73 loss to the University of Nevada at Las Vegas in the NCAA title game. But Duke's appearance in the title game was far from likely. Duke lost its last three regular-season ACC games to finish in second place in the conference and then lost to Georgia Tech in the ACC Tournament semifinals to drop out of the national top 10.

Senior guard Phil Henderson blasted his teammates in the locker room after the Tech game, calling them "a bunch of crybabies and quitters." Henderson's remarks sparked Duke to four wins in the NCAA Tournament and their third consecutive Final Four.

"Seasons can have defining moments, and this was a defining moment," Robert Brickey says. "We needed somebody to step up and be vocal, to spark a flame. We knew he was right."

Senior center Alaa Abdelnaby later admitted that he deserved the criticism. He lost his starting job for the first NCAA Tournament game against Richmond but came off the bench for 22 points. Abdelnaby would score 80 points in four Eastern Regional wins.

One at a Time?

Basketball coaches are fond of telling their team to catch up one possession at a time. After, all you can't score six points on one possession.

OR CAN YOU?

In 1990 Duke was trailing St. John's 61-53 with about nine minutes left in their second-round NCAA Tournament game. Duke lost possession of the ball, and St. John's Billy Singleton grabbed the loose ball. Duke's Robert Brickey stole the ball from Singleton, who tried to steal it back. Singleton was called for a personal foul and protested the call so vehemently that he was hit with a technical foul. A career 62-percent free throw shooter, Brickey made both ends of the one-and-one. He looked so composed at the line that Mike Krzyzewski decided to let him take the technicals.

"I was a little surprised that Coach K let me shoot the technicals," he said. "I looked over at the bench to see who was going to shoot the rest, and he pointed to me. I looked around to make sure he wasn't pointing at anyone else, and there was no one around but me."

Brickey made the two shots for the technical. Duke retained possession and Alaa Abdelnaby scored inside, giving Duke a six-point possession. Duke came back to win 76-72, with Brickey scoring the go-ahead points on an offensive rebound and sewing up the win with two free throws. The senior forward kept his career alive with 22 points.

"This just shows how attuned Coach K is to the ebb and flow of the game," Brickey adds 15 years later. "On paper, it didn't make sense to keep me at the line. But he could see that I was comfortable, that I was in rhythm, and he thought outside of the box and went with his instinct. And his instincts are almost always right."

SPECIAL

Duke and Connecticut squared off in the 1990 Eastern Regional finals. Duke trailed by a point with 2.6 seconds left in overtime but had the ball out of bounds on the Duke side of midcourt. Duke had a play designed for this situation called "Special." In this play, the player who receives the inbounds pass immediately throws it back to the passer, who takes the shot. Duke had planned to go inside to center Alaa Abdelnaby or set a screen for guard Phil Henderson, but Connecticut had them covered. Mike Krzyzewski saw this and screamed, "Special!" to Laettner, who was making the inbound pass, and Brian Davis, who was receiving the pass.

The two picked up the signal.

Laettner passed to Davis, quickly received the return pass, and made a 17-foot jump shot to win the game 78-77. The other three Duke players weren't in on the exchange and were running a completely different play.

GOING SOMEWHERE?

After the 1990 NBA season, Mike Krzyzewski was approached by the NBA's Boston Celtics. He gave the job serious consideration before turning it down.

"There are a lot of coaches who believe you shouldn't stay in a place more than six or seven years," he said. "I've never believed that in the past, but last year for the first time, I could see why guys might think that way. I looked at our team and thought our guys were doing a great job and yet people doubted them and questioned them. I didn't think that was fair. It frustrated me."

BOBBY HURLEY

Bobby Hurley was the prototypical point guard. A coach's son, skilled and cerebral, Hurley would record 1,076 assists, an NCAA record that has never been seriously challenged. Barely six feet tall, Hurley never used his lack of size as an excuse.

"I really like it when a team presses me with big guys. I stay low, and it's like I'm dribbling through cones. They might as well not be out there."

Bobby Hurley

"If you were where you were supposed to be, he would get you the ball," Greg Koubek says. "That simple. His court vision was extraordinary."

"I loved to run, and I really loved to run when Bobby had the ball in his hands," Robert Brickey says. "We all ran a little harder, knowing that there was a layup waiting for us at the other end."

Hurley led Duke to the national title game as a freshman. He had a stomach virus when Duke played UNLV. Hurley had a miserable game, and UNLV destroyed Duke 103-73. For months after the game Hurley had nightmares of sharks chasing him.

TOUGH LOVE

Sometimes seniors expect to play just because they are seniors. Greg Koubek was in that category in 1991 but wasn't playing well enough to get playing time. He contemplated quitting the team at midseason but changed his mind after a discussion with Mike Krzyzewski.

"Coach K was honest with me," Koubek recalls. "He went down the roster. 'Brian Davis? He's playing better than you. Thomas Hill? He's playing better than you. Billy McCaffrey? He's playing better than you.' I had to agree. They were. The message was quit feeling sorry for yourself and go out and earn some playing time."

Koubek rededicated himself to basketball. He not only earned playing time, but started down the stretch as Duke fought its way to its first national title.

LET'S PRACTICE

Duke made the long bus trip to Charlottesville, Virginia, on January 5, 1991, ranked eighth in the polls and boasting a five-game winning streak. The streak ended in a big way, as Duke was pounded 81-64.

"We didn't take the loss as seriously as we should have," Greg Koubek says. "There was too much laughing and joking on the bus ride back."

Duke got off the bus and found out that Mike Krzyzewski had called an immediate practice right then.

"We did lots of running," Koubek says. "Every time we had a turnover or messed up a play, we were sprinting from one end of the floor to the other. We thought of it as an attitude adjustment. Coach

K knew that something was wrong, and his reaction was to fix it right away."

Grant Hill ran into an inadvertent elbow in the practice and broke his nose, but the practice served its purpose. Duke pounded nationally ranked Georgia Tech 98-57 in its next game and went on a five-game winning streak.

THE MAN IN THE MASK

Grant Hill played several games with a mask protecting his broken nose. Duke did some experimenting, trying to find the right fit.

"I still have the mask at my parent's house," Hill says, "but I was pretty glad to take it off for the last time. It wasn't comfortable, I couldn't breathe right, and it made me look like a character from a horror movie."

In fact, opposing fans called him "Jason," after the movie villain.

WE'RE GONNA WIN

Duke captured the 1991 Atlantic Coast Conference regular-season championship and advanced to the ACC Tournament title game against North Carolina, a team Duke had beaten twice that season. The game was a horror show for Duke. The Devils played poorly, lost their composure, received several technical fouls, and lost 96-74.

The Duke players expected to be blasted by Mike Krzyzewski after the game. Instead they got a big surprise.

"Coach K came into the locker room and announced that we were going to win the national championship in three weeks," Marty Clark recalls. "He said we had gotten the bad game out of our system, and we were going to learn from it and put it behind us. It was a masterstroke of psychology. He took our minds from the poor game we had just played and immediately turned them toward the future, toward the NCAAs."

"Coach K has the remarkable ability to read his players, both individually and collectively," Greg Koubek adds. "He knew when we needed a kick in the pants and when we needed some encouragement. Somehow, he sensed that we didn't need to hear how badly we had played, we needed something else, and he gave us what we needed."

Grant Hill

THE RIVALRY

Duke and North Carolina each advanced to the 1991 Final Four but did not meet. In fact, the two powerhouse programs have never met in the NCAAs; they did play in the 1971 NIT.

"I can live with losing to any school," Mike Krzyzewski says. "But what would happen in this area, people-wise, if one of us beat the other in the championship game. That I wouldn't wish on anybody, it would be so horrible."

UNDERDOGS

Duke surprisingly had advanced to the 1990 NCAA title game against UNLV. The game had been close for about 30 minutes, but the Runnin' Rebels had run away from Duke down the stretch to win 103-73, still the largest margin ever in an NCAA title game.

The two teams again advanced to the Final Four the following season. UNLV was undefeated, ranked No. 1, and widely hailed as the best team since the UCLA juggernauts of the 1960s. No one gave Duke much of a chance.

"We were a little glum when we realized we were going to be playing UNLV again," Greg Koubek remembers. "We knew what they had done to us the year before. We thought of them as an NBA team."

Mike Krzyzewski had some selling to do. He used UNLV's dominance to his advantage. In the days leading up to the game he lavishly praised UNLV to the national media while telling his team to ignore his media buildup. Krzyzewski felt that Duke could keep the game close.

"If it's close at the end, it will be new for them," Krzyzewski explained. "They haven't been there. You have. Keep it close, and we'll win.

"There will come a time in this game when they will look into your eyes, and the game will be decided based on what they see."

"Coach K was so positive, so sure that he convinced us," Koubek says. "By game time we weren't afraid of anything or anybody."

KEEPING IT CLOSE

Mike Krzyzewski was right. Duke jumped to a 15-6 lead, but UNLV came back to tie the game 18-18. The Rebels led 43-41 at the half. The teams remained close throughout the second half. UNLV led by as many as five points late in the game, but they were in foul trouble. Bobby Hurley made a big three-point shot, and Brian Davis gave Duke a one-point lead with a three-point play inside. Larry Johnson tied the game 79-79 when he made one of two free throws. Duke's Thomas Hill missed a short jump shot, but Christian Laettner grabbed the rebound and was fouled. Laettner made both foul shots with 12.7 seconds left to give Duke a 79-77 lead.

Still, UNLV had plenty of time to send the game into overtime or even win it with a three-pointer. However, their point guard Greg Anthony had fouled out.

"We liked our position," Grant Hill says. "We always felt we could win a game on defense."

He was right. UNLV panicked against Duke's intense defense and forced up a shot that missed badly. Duke had slain Goliath.

"We realized right away that we had done something special, something for the ages," Hill explains.

NEW WEAPON

How could Duke lose to UNLV by 30 points, graduate three senior starters, and come back and beat essentially the same UNLV team a year later? Certainly, the improvement of players like Christian Laettner, Bobby Hurley, and Thomas Hill was crucial. But Duke's secret weapon was gifted freshman forward Grant Hill.

Greg Koubek remembers his first practice with Hill.

"I was a senior, so I figured I should start over any freshman, no matter how talented. One of our big defensive points of emphasis was to force the dribbler to the baseline, where they would be trapped. I tried this on Grant. He did a 180-degree spin and left me flat-footed. I turned around just in time to see him slam the ball through the goal. I realized at that point that if I was going to start, I was going to have to beat out somebody else. Nobody was going to keep Grant on the bench."

Hill subsumed his skills to the veterans, perhaps too much so. Mike Krzyzewski kept after him to be more selfish. By the Final Four, Hill had become an integral part of the Duke team. He took the opening tap against UNLV and drove in for an emphatic dunk, showing the favored Rebels that Duke wasn't backing down.

"This was a huge statement play for us," recalls Koubek, who had fought his way into the starting lineup. "In one play it took away all the negativity from the previous game against them, showed everybody that we weren't going to back down. We knew we were going to win."

FITTING IN

Mike Krzyzewski has claimed that Grant Hill was too unselfish early in his career. Hill isn't so sure.

"We had leaders in [Bobby] Hurley and [Christian] Laettner. I had a role to play, and that wasn't my role, not then. The way I look at it is we won two national titles. If I had been more assertive, it might have backfired, maybe we don't win."

ONE MORE TO GO

Duke's celebration at the end of the UNLV game was immediate and exuberant. But there was one dissenter. Mike Krzyzewski rushed onto the floor and tried to calm down the Duke players. As gratifying as the game was, it still was the national semifinal. Duke still had a game to go, and Krzyzewski was worried that Duke might not bring its customary intensity.

The next day Duke practiced in preparation for the title game against Kansas.

"We were a little full of ourselves, and Coach K could see it right away," Greg Koubek says. "He let us have it. He told us we hadn't done anything, and that we wouldn't beat Kansas if we didn't play with more hunger and passion. He made his point."

THAT'S BETTER

The Kansas game lacked the drama of the UNLV game, but it wasn't easy. Greg Koubek scored the game's first five points, and Duke never trailed. The Devils led 42-34 at the half and extended the lead to 14 midway through the half. Kansas rallied to within five points, but Duke held on for a 72-65 win.

After the game Mike Krzyzewski related a story from the previous year. After losing to UNLV in the title game, Krzyzewski's mother, Emily, told him, "Don't worry, you'll do better next year."

Krzyzewski explained to his mother how unlikely that was but kept coming back to that memory.

After the game Emily Krzyzewski looked her son in the face and said simply, "I told you so."

THE DUNK

The defining play in the 1991 title game was a spectacular dunk by Grant Hill early in the contest, a play that has been broadcast thousands of times in the ensuing 15 years. Bobby Hurley threw an errant lob pass that was headed for the stands when Hill somehow managed to corral it high in the air and slam it down for two points.

"I didn't realize it was anything special at the time," Hill says. "I just went back down the court and played defense. I remember thinking that it was a really bad pass from Bobby. Then I forgot about it."

TAKE IT AWAY?

On the first day of practice for the 1991-1992 season Mike Krzyzewski told his Duke team, "We are not defending a national title. We are pursuing a national title. I don't want to hear anyone use the word *defend.*"

Krzyzewski's position was that nothing that happened in 1992 would impact their 1991 title. It couldn't be taken away; therefore Duke wasn't defending it or anything else.

NOT TONIGHT

Duke was playing Georgia Tech at home in January 1992. Duke had a comfortable lead with about four minutes left when assistant coach Tommy Amaker turned to Mike Krzyzewski and suggested that Bobby Hurley looked tired and needed to come out. Krzyzewski wasn't convinced, but Amaker insisted. With the game in hand, Krzyzewski pulled Hurley out of the lineup and sat him down. It turned out that Hurley's seven assists that night gave him 707 for his Duke career. The school record was 708. It was held by Tommy

Amaker. Amaker's joke was successful, but after the game he admitted to the media that Hurley was "the best point guard in Duke history, and it's not even close."

Hurley got the record in the next game on an assist to Thomas Hill against North Carolina. Unfortunately, Hurley broke a bone in his right foot on the play. Duke lost to UNC 75-73, the first loss after 17 wins to open the season. Hurley would miss three weeks with the injury.

HOLD THAT TIGER

In 1992 Duke visited Baton Rogue to play Shaquille O'Neal and the LSU Tigers. Duke announcer Bob Harris remembers going by a tunnel on the way to the broadcast booth just before tipoff when a security guard stopped him. The LSU team was coming onto the floor.

"I looked into the tunnel, and Shaq was coming right at me. I backed as close to the wall as I could and felt something metallic at my back. I looked around and saw that I was pressed against the tiger cage, and Mike the Bengal Tiger had his eye on me. Shaq on one side and a tiger on the other. I stayed real still until it was clear and then got to my seat as fast as I could."

This was Duke's first game without Bobby Hurley. Grant Hill filled in at the point, Christian Laettner played O'Neal even, and Duke won a big road game 77-67. Best of all, Mike the Tiger didn't eat anyone.

Hill had played point guard in high school and sporadically at Duke when Hurley took a rare rest.

"I was comfortable at the point," Hill explains. "I felt prepared."

Duke was surprisingly smooth without Hurley, as the versatile Hill filled in with aplomb.

DRESS REHEARSAL NEEDS WORK

Duke only lost two games in 1992. The first was the game at UNC when Bobby Hurley broke his foot. The second was at Wake Forest.

Against Wake, Duke had a chance trailing 70-68 with only seconds left. Duke had the ball out of bounds under its own basket.

Mike Krzyzewski had been working on a play for exactly this situation. Grant Hill would throw a length-of-the-floor pass to

Christian Laettner just left of the other team's foul line. Laettner would catch the pass and take a quick jump shot. Given the distance involved, the margin of error was small.

Against Wake, Hill's pass had the right distance, but he threw a slight curveball. The pass carried Laettner to the edge of the floor, and he stepped on the baseline. Wake Forest made two free throws and won 72-68.

Duke would have another chance to run the same play a few weeks later.

CLEMSON UPSET AVOIDED

The powerful 1992 Duke team didn't have much to worry about from the Clemson Tigers. At least until they played them. The overconfident Devils traveled to Clemson on March 4 and just about had their heads handed to them. Clemson led 52-47 at the half and extended the lead to 68-51. A furious Mike Krzyzewski pulled his starters and put in reserves Cherokee Parks, Eric Meek, Marty Clark, Christian Ast, and Kenny Blakeney. The reserves exploded, running Clemson all over the court, pounding the ball inside and crashing the boards. The little-used Meek scored seven points in less than five minutes. Christian Laettner, Bobby Hurley, and Grant Hill became cheerleaders. Duke cut the lead to seven, the starters returned, and Duke pulled out a 98-97 win. Also claiming the hero's mantle was senior Brian Davis, who scored a career-high 30 points.

"We practiced a lot as a unit, so we felt comfortable together," Marty Clark says. "We figured we had an opportunity, so why not make advantage of it. I told Christian after the game that he owed us one."

Grant Hill, who sat out the Clemson game with a foot injury, maintains, "Close games like this helped us down the stretch. We needed some adversity to maintain our focus."

ROCK STARS

By the 1991-1992 season the Duke team had taken on the aura of rock stars. Opposing fans would root against Duke for two hours and then line up by the hundreds for autographs. After games at Maryland and Clemson, officials had to make arrangements to sneak Duke out by back exits.

"Crazy stuff like this happened all the time," Grant Hill says. "At the time we probably didn't realize how unusual it was, but we felt like it contributed to our mystique, our aura."

BROTHERS

Bob Hurley Sr. is one of the nation's most successful high school coaches. His St. Anthony's teams have sent numerous players into the college ranks, including sons Bobby Jr. and Danny, who played at Seton Hall. In 1992 Duke met Seton Hall in the third round of the NCAA Tournament. The Hurley parents elected to sit with the Duke fans, reasoning that Bobby was older than Danny and was thus deserving of their support.

Bobby had a miserable game, turning the ball over six times and scoring only four points. Duke still won 81-69. Hurley admitted that playing against his brother was "really distracting, the hardest thing I've had to do."

THE BEST EVER

What can be said about the 1992 Duke–Kentucky game for the Eastern Regional title? Two of basketball's most storied programs slugged it out more than 45 minutes, the game ending on the most unlikely shot in college basketball history.

Many in the Duke camp thought the semifinal game against Seton Hall—with its Hurley brothers subplot—would be the most difficult game in the Eastern Regionals. They were mistaken.

Kentucky made four three-pointers early and jumped to a 20-12 lead. A 15-2 Duke run put the Devils ahead. It was 50-45 at the half and 67-55 in the middle of the second half. But Kentucky relied heavily on three-point shots and a full-court press, the perfect recipe for coming from behind. They tied the game and sent it into overtime.

"It's gratifying to have played in a game that people remember so vividly," Grant Hill says. "But we felt like we had allowed Kentucky to make it a great game. Usually, when we got somebody on the ropes we put them away. We had control of the game and let them back in. Give them credit, but it shouldn't have come to that."

THE PASS

Duke practiced long baseball passes on a regular basis. Grant Hill threw the best pass, and he jokingly called himself the quarterback. The play hadn't worked earlier in the season against Wake Forest. On that occasion the play had been designed for Christian Laettner to catch the pass near the baseline. After Kentucky's Sean Woods had put the Wildcats up 103-102 with 2.1 seconds left, Mike Krzyzewski decided to try the same play but move Laettner to the middle of the floor. Kentucky coach Rick Pitino decided to double-team Laettner but leave Hill unguarded on the baseline. Hill's 80-foot pass was perfect. Laettner caught the pass, faked, dribbled, and buried the most famous jump shot in NCAA history for a 104-103 Duke win.

The shot capped a perfect shooting performance from the senior, 10 of 10 from the field, including one three-pointer, and 10 of 10 from the foul line, for 31 points.

What was Hill thinking before the pass?

"I have no idea," he says. "I was just blank. So much was going on. I just relied on training and instinct. It was just throw and hope."

MARTY CLARK

Sophomore forward Marty Clark had played about 200 minutes going into the 1992 Final Four game against Indiana. The Hoosiers jumped to a big lead early, but Bobby Hurley led a Duke surge with six three-point shots. Duke appeared to have a comfortable lead when Indiana mounted a late comeback.

Brian Davis hurt his knee late in the game, and then Grant Hill fouled out. Mike Krzyzewski looked down his bench to Clark.

"He looked right into my eyes and asked me if I was ready. I guess he liked what he saw."

Clark came in with Duke nursing a slim lead. Indiana went right after him. He was fouled three times in the final minute.

"It was not a place I expected to be," Clark says. "I was thrown into the fire. I remember not being able to feel very much in my arm and my legs. I short-armed the first one, but it crawled over the rim and I was alright."

Clark made five of six free throws, and Duke survived for an 81-78 win.

BACK TO BACK

Duke was matched in the title game against Michigan and its five freshmen starters, the Fab Five. Michigan had carried Duke into overtime earlier that season at home before losing and felt confident that they could handled the favored Devils this time. Michigan freshman star Chris Webber told everyone, "It's payback time." For 20 minutes it looked like Webber might have been right. Brian Davis was still injured and Christian Laettner struggled in the first half, turning the ball over seven times. Duke trailed by one at the half.

Duke regrouped at intermission.

"We had played poorly, but we were only behind by a point," Grant Hill says. "We knew if we played smarter and harder, we would win."

Duke did exactly that. Laettner responded with 14 second-half points, and Duke pulled away for a 71-51 win.

BACK TO BACK

Duke's 1991 and 1992 titles make them the only program to repeat since the NCAA Tournament expanded to its modern form in the 1970s.

"We were really pretty confident, with great senior leaders, and it still was almost too much for us," Grant Hill explains. "The pressure is unrelenting, the expectations never let up. It wears you out. It requires so much energy. At the end of the 1991 season we were exultant. At the end of the 1992 season we were more relieved than anything else."

HURLEY BOWS OUT

1993 was a Bobby Hurley's year. With Christian Laettner gone, Hurley increased his scoring to 17 points per game. Late in the season he became the NCAA career leader in assists; he ended with 1,076, still a record. A serious toe injury to Grant Hill in midseason ended any realistic chance for another Duke title. The season ended in the second round of the NCAA Tournament with an 82-77 loss to Jason Kidd and California. Hurley kept Duke in the game, with a career-high 32 points. The loss ended Duke's run of five consecutive Final Fours and the school's 13-game NCAA win streak.

After the game Mike Krzyzewski lauded Hurley and fellow senior Thomas Hill.

"They've taken me places, and I've had experiences no other college coach has had over the last 20 years. Every time they went on the court, I knew they'd give me their bodies, their minds, and their hearts."

GRANT HILL

Just as 1993 had been Bobby Hurley's year, 1994 was Grant Hill's season. Duke called their offense that year the "Ride Grant's Back" offense. Mike Krzyzewski joked that Duke was working to perfect a play where Hill passed the ball to himself.

"We knew we were riding Grant and would go as far as he could take us," teammate Marty Clark says.

Hill took Duke to the ACC regular-season title, scoring, rebounding, passing, and playing defense at a high level. More importantly, he provided leadership.

"He kept us calm; he kept us focused," Clark says. "The other team was concentrating on him, so that opened up the floor for the rest of us. He recognized that and took advantage of it. It wasn't our best team, but it was our most cohesive. It was a fun year."

"He wasn't a talk-a-lot leader," freshman Jeff Capel says. "His leadership was more subtle. He led by example. Grant took me under his wing immediately and showed me how hard he worked, what I would have to do to become an ACC-caliber player. He did that for everybody. People tried to get him to shoot more, to pad his scoring average. His response was that it was more important to help develop the team because he would need us down the road. I'll always remember how he sublimated his game, his ego, and concentrated on helping his teammates grow."

SHUTTING UP THE "BIG DOG"

Purdue forward Glenn "Big Dog" Robinson won all the major Player of the Year awards in 1994. It made sense. Robinson averaged 30 points per game for a team that entered the NCAA Tournament ranked third. But Grant Hill wasn't sure. He chafed a little. He thought he had a better all-around game than Robinson. When Duke and Purdue met in the Midwest Regional finals that year, Hill showed why he felt that way. He held Robinson to 13 points, and Duke upset the Boilermakers 69-60.

"This was Grant's finest hour," Jeff Capel says. "But I also remember when Grant sat down with four fouls and we maintained the lead. He had told everybody that Duke would need us, and when that time arrived, we were ready. Then he came back in and closed the deal."

Hill carried Duke all the way to the title game against Arkansas, where the Razorbacks' superior depth wore down Duke 76-72.

Duke's appearance in the 1994 title game ended a decade of dominance. Duke had appeared in 11 consecutive NCAA Tournaments, had made seven of the last nine Final Fours, and had captured two national titles. The next few years would see Duke briefly fall back in the pack before regaining the top.

Chapter 6

MIKE KRZYZEWSKI RELOADS

A LOST SEASON

The 1994-1995 season is one that Duke basketball fans prefer to forget. It got off to a bad start when Duke cancelled a late-spring trip to Australia because of poor academic performance by several of the freshmen. It got worse. Mike Krzyzewski had been bothered by a disc in his back for much of the 1994 season. Assorted treatments didn't alleviate the problem, and he had surgery on October 23, shortly after the opening of practice.

Krzyzewski was advised to take off six to eight weeks to allow for full recovery. He came back in 10 days. He was in constant pain and was unable to sleep for more than a few hours at a time. In early January Duke was upset at home by Clemson to drop its record to 9-3. Krzyzewski was unable to continue.

Veteran assistant Pete Gaudet replaced Krzyzewski as interim coach. Duke lost 15 of its 19 games under Gaudet. Eight of the losses were by five or fewer points, including home losses to Virginia and North Carolina in double overtime. Duke ended its season 13-18, the most losses in school history. That was the only season since 1983 that Duke has not played in the NCAA Tournament.

WHAT HAPPENED?

How can a program go from playing for the NCAA title one year to last place in the ACC the following season?

"First, you can't blame Pete Gaudet," Jeff Capel says, "He was thrown into an impossible situation, trying to replace the best coach in the country practically overnight. Maybe we relied too much on Coach K. Without him on the bench, we just didn't have the confidence. We started splintering, looking around, wondering what was going to happen next. Every close game we would start thinking that bad things were going to happen and we couldn't stop the slide."

DUKE–UNC CLASSIC

"When these two great rivals meet, you can throw away the record books." This is sportswriting cliché No. 1. But occasionally the cliché comes true.

In early February 1995 North Carolina made the brief trip to Durham to take on Duke. On paper the game was a total mismatch. North Carolina was 16-1 and was ranked second in the country. Duke was 0-7 in the ACC and had lost seven of its previous eight contests. When UNC made its first eight field goals and jumped to a 26-9 lead, it looked like the rout was on. But Duke fought back. Senior Cherokee Parks battled UNC inside while freshman Trajan Langdon made five three-pointers. Duke closed to within five at the half and spurted to a 68-56 lead with 9:52 left only to see UNC tie the game and force an overtime.

Then it got interesting. UNC jumped to a 90-81 lead, but again Duke fought back. A barrage of three-pointers made the score 95-92 with four seconds left. UNC's Serge Zwikker had a chance to sew up the game but missed two free throws. Duke's Jeff Capel launched a shot just inside the midcourt line as the buzzer sounded. It swished through the nets, sending the game into a second overtime.

The second overtime was close and hard-fought. Duke had two shots in the final seconds to send the game into a third overtime but missed both and lost 102-100.

After the game an incredulous Dean Smith remarked, "I've never seen anything like it. If you don't like this, you don't like college basketball."

"Everybody thinks that shot won the game," says Capel, now the coach at Virginia Commonwealth. "They're astonished when I tell them we actually lost the game. That's the play that everybody remembers me for, and they remember it wrong."

BUILDING A BRIDGE

Mike Krzyzewski returned to the ACC wars for the 1995-1996 season. It was a rocky return. Duke started the season by winning the Great Alaska Shootout and returned to the national polls. But guard Trajan Langdon missed the entire season with a leg injury. Senior forward Tony Moore became academically ineligible at midseason. Four other players missed games because of injuries down the stretch, including star senior guard Chris Collins. Duke eked back into the NCAA Tournament but depleted by injuries lost its first game and finished the season at 18-13. Krzyzewski has referred to this team as a "bridge team" between the dominance of the 1986-1994 era and the dominance to come.

CHRIS COLLINS

Chris Collins was one of the few bright spots in the 1996 season. Collins is the son of former NBA star and coach Doug Collins. Chris started for the 1994 Duke team but broke his foot early in the 1994-1995 season and never fully recovered. Collins was a fiery player, passionate and enthusiastic, with a shooting range that extended almost to midcourt. His 30 points against Iowa keyed Duke to the 1995 Great Alaska Shootout title, which returned Duke to the national polls.

Collins ended his career on a down note. He sprained an ankle in the regular-season finale against North Carolina and missed the ACC Tournament, where Duke lost its first game. He tried to come back for the NCAA opener against Eastern Michigan but could only play a few minutes in Duke's 75-60 loss.

TWO BOUNCES

Chris Collins' biggest basket came in Raleigh, in mid-January. Duke had lost its first four ACC games, three by five or fewer points, and badly needed a win. Duke trailed North Carolina State 70-68 with seconds left when Duke brought the ball downcourt. Collins was supposed to pass the ball to Ricky Price on a play called a dribble exchange.

"The times I did that before, my man and his man both went with the him," Collins remembers. "I saw they were going to do it again, I just kept it on the fake and took the shot."

Some shot it was. From 30 feet out it hit the front of the rim, bounced up to the backboard, dropped down, bounced twice more, and dropped through. Duke was up 71-70 with 5.5 seconds left.

"Not only did he not do what he was supposed to do, but he almost stepped on my toe," coach Mike Krzyzewski said. "But I'll take it."

Still, the game was not over. State quickly threw the ball in to Curtis Marshall, who raced up the court and tossed up a contested five-footer. It bounced around and bounced off. Duke's Steve Wojciechowski had a great view of both shots.

"From my angle, I was sure that Chris' shot was short, and I was sure that Marshall's shot was in," he says. "Usually, I hate to be proven wrong, but not this time."

Two bounces, two results. Duke used the momentum of the win to capture eight of its final 12 ACC games and make the NCAA Tournament. State faded from an 11-4 start to a 15-16 finish, and head coach Les Robinson was fired after the season.

UNCLE MATT

Few recent Duke players have had a more interesting journey than Matt Christensen. A 6-foot-10 center from Massachusetts, Christensen was Mike Krzyzewski's first signee after his back injury. Hampered by injuries, he played sparingly in 1995-1996. Christensen then spent two years in Germany on a Mormon mission. He came back for the 1999 season but redshirted. Christensen thus finished his career in the spring of 2002, almost seven years after arriving in Durham. By this time Christensen's teammates were calling him "Uncle Matt," and former teammates Chris Collins and Steve Wojciechowski were now Duke assistants.

EMPTY THE BENCH

There comes a time in most basketball games when the losing coach concedes and empties the bench. In Duke's March 1996 game against North Carolina, that point came with 1:04 left and Duke trailing 80-67. Mike Krzyzewski put in four walk-ons and the seldom-used Matt Christensen. Todd Singleton scored twice for

Duke, Baker Perry added a three-point shot, North Carolina missed some free throws, and the Duke scrubs went on a quick 9-1 run. With 18.2 seconds left, the score was 81-76 and Duke sent its starters back in. North Carolina finally quelled the rally with three free throws and held on for an 84-76 win.

With 26 seconds left, Duke's 5-foot-8, 150-pound Jay Heaps—an All-America soccer player and future professional soccer star— knocked North Carolina's volatile Jeff McInnis into the stands. Heaps was called for an intentional foul, the furious McInnis was called for his second technical foul and ejected, and Cameron Indoor Stadium erupted into pandemonium.

"I think McInnis was taken back by our intensity," Christensen says. "What did they expect? Maybe they thought we were going to play out the string, to go through the motions. But Duke never goes through the motions."

BACK ON TOP

Duke returned to national prominence in 1997. Guards Jeff Capel, Trajan Langdon, and Steve Wojciechowski gave Duke an outstanding perimeter game, while transfer Roshown McLeod and freshman Chris Carrawell manned the forward spots.

Center was a problem area, however. Sophomore Taymon Domzalski missed most of the season with injuries. Senior Greg Newton started strong. His 21-point, 13-rebound effort keyed Duke's overtime win over Florida State in December. But Newton began slumping in midseason. Soon he lost his starting job and then gradually disappeared from the playing rotation entirely.

Absent quality size, coach Mike Krzyzewski reinvented his team. Carrawell, only 6-foot-6, began playing center. Duke upset second-ranked Wake Forest and Tim Duncan 73-68 in Winston-Salem with Carrawell guarding Duncan. Duke squeezed out an 11-5 ACC mark, good for first place in the regular season. But the undersized Devils ran out of gas. They were upset by North Carolina State in the first round of the ACC Tournament and lost in the second round of the NCAAs to Providence. Still, Duke's 24-9 mark demonstrated that they were close to regaining the lofty national spot they had recently lost.

ROSHOWN MCLEOD

Mike Krzyzewski has long been wary of bringing in transfers from other programs. In the fall of 1994, forward Joey Beard announced that he was leaving Duke for Boston University. About the same time St. John's sophomore Roshown McLeod announced that he was leaving that school. McLeod had played high school ball for Bob Hurley Sr. and his recommendation helped convince Krzyzewski to go after the 6-foot-8 forward.

McLeod was a starter for two seasons and ended his Duke career as an All-ACC player.

Jeff Capel talks about 1996, the year McLeod had to sit out because of transfer rules.

"It was tough for Roshown. We really didn't have a tradition of transfers, so no one was sure what to do. Ro would practice, but he couldn't play and he couldn't travel. Practices were his games. He worked hard to help make his team better even though he had no short-term benefits. That showed me something."

THEY DON'T DO THAT HERE

Duke fans have a history of making life miserable for officials and for opposing players and coaches. They rarely turn on their own. But it does happen. On December 5, 1996, Duke hosted Florida State. Senior guard Jeff Capel had a miserable game, missing all nine of his field goal attempts and going scoreless. Mike Krzyzewski put Capel back in the game late, a decision met with an audible groan and some scattered boos. Duke won the game 72-66 in overtime.

"I was really excited by the win and the fact that my classmates Greg Newton and Carmen Wallace [13 points, 11 rebounds] had played well," Capel says. "But the more I thought about the fans, the worse I felt. They just don't do that stuff at Duke. For the only time in my career, I went out the back way to avoid the fans. I called my parents and told them not to come to the next home game. It hurt. I felt sorry for myself. I thought I was being held up as a scapegoat. But my teammates supported me; my coaches supported me. I   wasn't going to give up."

Capel didn't give up. He rebounded to play some of the best basketball of his career. Capel regained a starting spot in late January in time to score 19 points against North Carolina and help Duke break a seven-game losing streak against their rivals. Capel closed strong, averaging more than 20 points per game for his last five games.

WHISTLE? WHAT WHISTLE?

The ACC has had some bizarre finishes, but few match what happened in Charlottesville, Virginia, on February 11, 1997. Virginia's Norm Nolan went to the foul line with five seconds left and his team tied with Duke 60-60. Nolan missed the first of his two foul shots. After the first miss Virginia's Willie Dersch went to the scorer's table. Lead official Rick Hartzell was informed that Dersch would come in for Nolan if Nolan made the second free throw. Nolan did just that. The horn sounded, and Dersch prepared to enter the game. Hartzell, however, forgot the earlier conversation and did not acknowledge the horn. The ball was placed in play, and Jeff Capel inbounded to Steve Wojciechowski. The result was bedlam. The clock didn't start, Dersch was jumping up and down on the sidelines, and Virginia's Harold Deane was frantically pointing at the clock. Meanwhile, Wojciechowski was pushing the ball upcourt. He was eventually fouled.

It took some six minutes to straighten the situation out. The officials ruled that this was a non-correctable error. The final seconds were timed on a monitor, and the officials determined that 4.3 seconds had elapsed before the foul. The clock was set to 0.7 seconds. Wojciechowski made both foul shots, and Duke won 62-61.

"I knew we weren't going to call a timeout," Capel says. "We practice that play all the time, throwing the ball in quickly and pushing it down the floor. I knew that Dersch was ready to come in, and I expected to hear the whistle but threw the ball in anyway. I wasn't trying to steal a play or anything, it was just instinct. I can see it today like it's in slow motion, the perplexed look on Deane's face, the desperate foul, everything. Certainly, the strangest moment of my basketball career."

Mike Krzyzewski acknowledged, "We were fortunate. I don't want to win by any shenanigans—wins aren't that important. But this isn't Cameron. We made winning plays."

Hartzell and his crew were reprimanded and suspended for one ACC game, an unprecedented action for a mistake that Hartzell acknowledged as "one I will carry to my grave."

REINFORCEMENTS

Mike Krzyzewski knew that he needed size for the 1997-1998 season. By the middle 1990s basketball recruiting had become a spectator sport. The advent of high-profile, invitation-only summer camps for high school players, professional recruiting gurus, and the Internet meant that basketball aficionados closely followed the recruiting ups and downs of their favorite teams. Thus, when Krzyzewski brought in three front-court players ranked in the top 10, it was front-page news. Two of these recruits, Elton Brand and Shane Battier, would go on to become consensus national players of the year. Chris Burgess would play two seasons for Duke before transferring to Utah. Guard William Avery would become an All-ACC and NBA player.

DUKE'S LEVEL

From 1998 through 2005 Duke dominated the ACC as no team had ever done before or since. Duke finished in first place in the regular season six times in this eight-year period. Duke made the finals of the ACC Tournament all eight years, winning six. From 1998 through 2000 Duke won 46 of 48 ACC regular-season contests. Duke's dominance gave rise to the ABD club, Anybody But Duke, as rival fans grew weary of long losing streaks against Duke.

Wake Forest coach Dave Odom put it in perspective in 2000.

"It's not up to Duke to come down to our level, it's up to us to rise to Duke's level."

ELTON BRAND

Elton Brand had a lot to do with those winning streaks. A powerful but quick 6-foot-8, 260-pound forward/center from Peekskill, New York, Brand immediately won the starting job at center in the fall of 1997. He was a dominant force inside before breaking a foot during a late-December practice. Mike Krzyzewski told his team that Brand was out for the season.

"We didn't want them waiting for him to come back," he said. "We never talked about Elton's injury. We just went out and played."

Duke continued to win and reached number one in the polls without Brand. The freshman healed in time to return for the last weeks of the season, although he didn't regain his pre-injury form.

DARK ALLEYS?

Duke went to Chapel Hill on February 5, 1998, ranked number one. They left on the short end of a 97-73 score. The rematch was three weeks later on the final weekend of the regular season. UNC continued its dominance of Duke for much of the game. With 11:39 left they led Duke 64-47.

Elton Brand was playing in his third game since returning from a broken foot. The precocious freshman led a riveting comeback. He muscled inside for eight points in less than three minutes. Then North Carolina began committing turnovers. Chris Carrawell tied the game 75-75, and Roshown McLeod gave Duke a 77-75 lead, Duke's first lead of the game. North Carolina's Ed Cota was fouled with 3.8 seconds left, but he missed the first free throw and missed the second on purpose. Teammate Brendan Haywood gathered the rebound and was fouled. Haywood also missed both free throws, and Duke escaped with a 77-75 win.

Senior McLeod led Duke with 23 points, while Brand added 16. The unsung hero was senior Steve Wojciechowski, who scored only a single point but dished out 11 assists and provided fiery leadership in the comeback. Just under 6 feet tall, a mediocre shooter, and a limited athlete, "Wojo" may have gotten more out of his innate ability that any player in Duke history. He used his intelligence and his desire to win the National Defensive Player of the Year award in 1997. After the UNC game, Mike Krzyzewski summed up Wojo's contributions to Duke.

"I'll take my point guard down any alley, down any dark street. He's the best leader we've ever had."

The win was Krzyzewski's 500th as a college coach.

TRAJAN LANGDON

Duke has gone great distances to secure the talents of its basketball players but never as far as it did when Mike Krzyzewski convinced Trajan Langdon to come to Durham. Langdon played his high school basketball in Anchorage, Alaska. A 6-foot-3 guard, the cool and

Elton Brand

cerebral Langdon would be known as the "Alaskan Assassin" for the methodical way he destroyed opponents. Langdon was a deadly three-point shooter, with a remarkable quick release. He was named first-team All-ACC three times, 1997, 1998, and 1999, the only player to accomplish that feat during Krzyzewski's tenure at Duke.

BACK WHERE WE WANTED TO BE

Duke entered the 1998 NCAA Tournament as a top seed and proceeded to defeat Radford, Oklahoma State, and Syracuse to advance to the finals of the South Regional against second-seeded Kentucky. Duke led by 17 points in the second half before a barrage of Kentucky three-pointers and Duke turnovers turned around the game. Kentucky came back for an 84-82 win, ending Duke's season at 32-4. This was the only time Duke has lost a Regional Final under Mike Krzyzewski.

Although obviously disappointed with the outcome, Krzyzewski saw the glass as half full.

"I couldn't be too down," he later observed. "In my mind we had won. We were back where we wanted to be, back to competing for a national title."

ALASKA

Many programs try to schedule a home game near their players' hometowns at least once during a career. That's not easy to do when you have a star player from Alaska. Duke played in the Great Alaska Shootout in Trajan Langdon's hometown of Anchorage at the beginning of the 1995-1996 season, but Langdon sat out that season with a leg injury. Duke tried again three years later. Duke went into the tournament ranked number one but lost to Cincinnati in the title game 77-75.

"The team was devastated," Matt Christensen says. "You always want to win for your seniors, the guys who have persevered over the years, but Trajan was special. It went beyond kinship. It was the most disappointing regular-season loss I can remember."

WHO IS THIS GUY?

Matt Christensen redshirted the 1998-1999 season after spending two years in Germany. He had not been allowed to play full-court basketball and knew that he would need some time to get back into playing shape. It's not like he took off the season, however. He got to practice every day against Elton Brand.

"I really didn't know much about Brand," Christensen says. "I had been away for a while. But I found out real quick. He was what we call 'Old-Man Strong.' Put him in a weight room, and nothing special happened. Put him on a basketball court, and he was the strongest guy I ever played against. You couldn't move him; you couldn't strip the ball from him; he had a high release, so you couldn't block his shot; and he was amazingly quick for his size. He could pretty much do whatever he wanted on the court."

JUGGERNAUT

The 1999 Duke team was a behemoth. Each of the starters—Elton Brand, Shane Battier, Chris Carrawell, Trajan Langdon, and William Avery—made All-ACC that year, the only time that has happened. Brand was ACC and National Player of the Year. Carrawell and Battier would later be ACC players of the year. Langdon joined Brand on the All-America teams.

After a two-point loss to Cincinnati in Alaska, Duke went undefeated in December, January, and February. Duke once led Michigan 34-2, won all 16 ACC regular-season games, and captured the ACC Tournament, defeating North Carolina by 23 points in the title game. Duke outscored its opponents by 24.6 points per game, a school and ACC record.

NEXT TO JEFFERSON

The 1999 Duke team defeated Virginia three times, by margins of 46, 46, and 37 points.

"If Taymon Domzalski played here, they'd build a monument to him on campus, right next to Thomas Jefferson," claimed an incredulous Virginia coach Pete Gillen after one loss. "There he can't even get into a game. That's ridiculous."

Domzalski was Duke's ninth man that season.

TURNING ON A SWITCH

Duke finished its 1999 home season with a game against Clemson. Duke was flat at the start, and the game was tied 30-30 with just under eight minutes left in the first half. Duke senior Trajan Langdon came off a screen and was blasted by a vicious Clemson forearm. Langdon lay on the floor for several minutes, bleeding profusely from the mouth. He was helped to the locker room; Clemson scored to take the lead. Then Duke scored. And scored. And scored again. Twenty-six unanswered points turned the close game into a rout.

"Seeing Trajan down turned on a switch for us," Chris Carrawell says. "We went off. It was show no mercy."

Langdon received several stitches and returned in the second half, scoring 17 points for the game. Duke won 92-65.

Mike Krzyzewski was asked after the game about his angry response to the foul.

"My captain was lying on the floor, bleeding. If I'm not emotional, somebody else needs to sit in the chair."

TOO GOOD?

Duke cruised through the early part of the 1999 postseason. The Devils won the ACC Tournament by margins of 37, 15, and 23 points, and captured the Eastern Regionals by margins of 41, 41, 17, and 21 points.

In the end this dominance may have hurt Duke. Duke survived second-ranked Michigan State 68-62 in a physical game to advance to the NCAA title game against third-ranked Connecticut.

JUST SHORT

Duke went into the 1999 national title game ready to be crowned as one of the best team's in college basketball history. But their opponent, Connecticut, was a skilled and experienced team that had spent as much of the season ranked No. 1 as Duke had. Connecticut effectively double-teamed Elton Brand, holding him to eight field-goal attempts. William Avery, Chris Carrawell, Shane Battier, and Corey Maggette all missed more than half of their shots.

Only Trajan Langdon was on his game. Playing his final game, the senior scored 25 points and made five three-pointers. Langdon had a chance to win the game late but lost the ball after being bumped by a defender. Connecticut made two free throws and won the title 77-74.

Mike Krzyzewski was criticized for not calling timeout but noted that this tactic had been successful in the past.

"That's the way we play," the coach explained. "We were going for the win."

MASS EXODUS

Duke fans could console themselves after the 1999 season with the expectation that the 2000 team would be even better. Trajan Langdon was the only key senior on the 1999 team, and another bumper crop of freshmen was coming in to augment the returnees.

This assurance didn't last long. Before 1999 Duke had never lost a player to the NBA draft prior to his senior season. Elton Brand became the first, announcing his intentions for the NBA just weeks after the 1999 title game. This was a big loss but not unexpected. Brand was regarded as the nation's top player and would be the first pick in the 1999 NBA draft. More surprising was the loss of sophomore guard William Avery and freshman forward Corey Maggette, both of whom would be selected in the middle of the first round.

Matt Christensen says he wasn't really surprised.

"Elton, William, and Corey were real tight. They did everything together. It made sense for Elton to leave. Once that happened, it made it more likely that William would leave, which made it more likely that Corey would leave. It just cascaded."

In addition, reserve center Chris Burgess announced that he was transferring to Utah.

CHRIS CARRAWELL'S SENIOR SEASON

Duke was left with only three returning players from the 1999 juggernaut, Shane Battier, Chris Carrawell, and Nate James, while Matt Christensen began playing again after his redshirt year. Carrawell was the key. Called "a magnificent warrior" by Mike Krzyzewski, the senior captain had been raised in a rough neighborhood in St. Louis and brought that toughness to every game he played at Duke. He had been the consummate role player for his first three seasons at Duke. In 1997, his freshman season, Carrawell played some center, despite being only 6-foot-6. In 1999, he was Duke's backup point guard. He routinely guarded the opposition's best perimeter scorer.

Duke began the 1999-2000 seasons with a pair of losses in New York, to Stanford and Connecticut, the first time Duke had lost its first two games in a season since 1958-1959. Duke responded to the setbacks with an 18-game winning streak, which included four wins in overtime.

Christensen gives Carrawell the lion's share of the credit.

"By the time he was a senior, he had played center against Tim Duncan, he had played point guard, he had been in so many big games. He was so confident. His attitude was, 'Been there, done that.' His cool under pressure made us believers. We trusted him to take us places."

Despite a series of injuries and illnesses, Duke lost only once in the ACC, going 15-1 in the regular season and winning the tournament. Duke advanced to the third round of the NCAA Tournament before losing to Florida.

SHANE BATTIER

Shane Battier epitomized the student-athlete. An exceptional student, Battier was named an Academic All-American. He alternately delighted the media by talking everything from economic theory to the subtitles of eastern religions during interviews. Battier interned on Wall Street and on Capitol Hill and was chairman of the National Association of Basketball Coaches' Student Basketball Council.

"Shane had incredible curiosity," Matt Christensen says. "He was one of the few people who could have a conversation with absolutely anyone and be interested in what they were saying."

At times his interests threatened to overwhelm him. Mike Krzyzewski noted that Battier was "one of those guys who feels like he's got a term paper due every day."

He first earned his stripes as a defensive specialist. He was named National Defensive Player of the Year in 1999, 2000, and 2001, the only player to ever win that award three times. After Duke lost its top four scorers following the 1999 season, Battier developed into a potent scorer.

"People don't realize how hard Shane worked to develop his game," Christensen says. "He was very analytical about it. When it was his time to lead, he was ready."

THE MICKIE-D'S

Chris Carrawell, Shane Battier, and Nate James were joined by another heralded group of freshmen. Jason Williams, Carlos Boozer, Mike Dunleavy, and Casey Sanders were all named to the prestigious McDonald's All-America team in high school, making Duke the only school to bring in four "Mickie-D's" in one recruiting class. Sanders never developed into more than a role player, but the other three all became top college players.

JASON WILLIAMS

Evaluating high school players is not an exact science as illustrated by the decision made by North Carolina coach Bill Guthridge in the summer of 1999. North Carolina was one of favorites for New Jersey prep sensation Jason Williams before Guthridge told Williams that the school wouldn't be recruiting him because "you can't score as well as we thought you could." Williams ended up at Duke, where he "had a chip on my shoulder" over Guthridge's snub. Duke won seven of eight games against North Carolina while Williams was at Duke. Williams, by the way, would lead the ACC in scoring in 2001 and 2002.

Williams was thrown into the fire. With the exodus of 1999, Williams was the only true guard on the 2000 team's regular rotation. He played almost every second and had the ball in his hands almost the entire time.

"It took him a little while to adjust to the heat of the spotlight," Matt Christensen says. "He tried to do too much, and sometimes his body language showed how frustrated he was. But when he got it, he got it. He was so talented and so explosive that you always felt that something marvelous was about to happen. You just held your breath."

THE FIRST 39 MINUTES DON'T GO WELL

Duke has been on both sides of some great comebacks. But few equal what happened at College Park, Maryland, on January 27, 2001, when the second-ranked Devils were visiting the eighth-ranked Terrapins. Maryland led 44-29 late in first half and maintained a similar margin for most of the second half. With 65 seconds left Maryland led 89-77, the Maryland fans were chanting, "Overrated!" at Duke, and ESPN had already named Maryland guard Steve Blake as the Player of the Game. Blake's selection made sense. He had played a solid floor game and had hounded Duke's Jason Williams into 10 turnovers and a miserable shooting performance.

THE LAST MINUTE GOES BETTER

Steve Blake fouled out with less than two minutes to play, and Maryland's ballhandling became shaky. Duke's Nate James made a three-pointer to cut the margin to nine, 89-80. A Maryland free throw extended the lead to seven. Then came the Jason Williams explosion. With 53 seconds left, he made a layup to make the score 90-82. He then stole the inbound pass and hit a three-pointer. Suddenly it was 90-85 with 48.5 seconds left. The rattled Terrapins missed two free throws, and Williams hit another three. It was 90-88 with 40.4 seconds left, and Williams had outscored Maryland 8-0 in 13 seconds. James stole an inbound pass and rebounded a Mike Dunleavy miss. James was fouled. A Maryland native, James calmly sank both free throws to tie the game 90-90 with 21.9 seconds left. Maryland held the ball for the last shot and missed.

Shane Battier dominated the overtime, scoring six points and blocking a Juan Dixon shot at the buzzer that could have tied the game. Duke won 98-96.

The aftermath of the game was controversial. Duke players and fans, including some players' parents, were hit with debris, including water bottles.

Asked about the "Overrated!" cheer after the game, Williams smiled and noted, "I hate that cheer."

Jason Williams

A NEW TEAM

Duke's second game against Maryland was also memorable. Center Carlos Boozer broke a bone in his right foot early in the second half, and Duke lost the game 91-80. Boozer's injury occurred at the end of February, perhaps too late in the season for his return. It appeared to most that Duke's national title hopes were as broken as Boozer's foot.

Mike Krzyzewski's initial reaction was that was the end of Duke's national title aspirations. After a sleepless night, he decided to dramatically retool the team. Slender but speedy center Casey Sanders would replace Boozer. Super-quick freshman guard Chris Duhon would replace senior Nate James in the lineup. Quickness would become the order of the day. Duke would increase defensive pressure while forcing the tempo on offense in an attempt to wear down bigger but slower opponents.

Krzyzewski broke this news to the team at a 6 a.m. practice and told his team that they would win the national championship if they believed in him and did what he told them.

"We were pretty down," Matt Christensen says. "At first, we weren't sure what to believe. We thought this was pretty late in the game to remake a team. But Coach kept emphasizing the positives. By the time of the North Carolina game, we had come around. We believed it."

PUTTING IT TO THE TEST

Duke may have believed, but most observers thought that Duke's season had come to a crashing halt.

"I kind of liked it because we were underdogs," Jason Williams says. "Being at Duke, I was never in a position where I was an underdog before. That was the first time."

Duke traveled to UNC for the regular-season finale with first place at stake.

Mike Krzyzewski's plan worked exactly as predicted. Duke forced North Carolina into turnovers, which were converted into easy baskets at the other end. Duke made 14 three-pointers. UNC's huge center Brendan Haywood became so exhausted by the quick tempo that he was reduced to walking across halfcourt. Duke won 95-81.

The two teams met one week later for the ACC Tournament title. Duke was even more dominant this time, completely shutting down North Carolina's offense and winning 79-53.

GOING FOR THREE

Mike Krzyzewski was originally opposed to the three-point shot. He thought it was too short, and he felt that the rule change was introduced over the objections of coaches. But he adapted. Oh, how he adapted. Duke consistently has been the one of the best three-point shooting teams in the country. The 2001 team made 407 three-point shots, an average of 10.5 per game. This remains an NCAA record. Jason Williams made 132 that season, Shane Battier 124, and Mike Dunleavy, Chris Duhon, and Nate James all made more than 40. Duke made 18 three-pointers twice that season and attempted 38 shots three times for school records that still stand.

Jeff Capel ranks sixth on Duke's career three-point shooter's list.

"This is another example of how Coach K can adjust and adapt," Capel explains. "Once the three-point shot became a reality, he realized he could either be beaten by it or use it to beat other teams. Not only does he always have a good three-point shooter on the floor, he usually has two, three, even four. He's made it a strength."

BOOZER'S FOOT

Carlos Boozer broke his right foot on February 27, 2001. Early projections were that he would miss the remainder of the season. The Duke medical staff did its work, Boozer kept in shape as best he could, and he returned to limited action in Duke's third NCAA Tournament game. Duke was undefeated in his absence, and Mike Krzyzewski demanded that Boozer "adjust to the way we were now playing—not the other way around." Boozer was more than happy to comply, coming off the bench the remainder of the season. Duke defeated UCLA and Southern California to advance to the Final Four.

WAIT, I KNOW THESE GUYS

Duke met Maryland for the third time in 2001 in the semifinals of the ACC Tournament. Duke led most of the game but needed a late tap-in by Nate James to escape with an 84-82 win. After four wins, both teams advanced to the Final Four. They met in the first game, the only time that Duke has ever played another ACC team in any NCAA Tournament.

Duke fell behind 39-17, a result both of Maryland's brilliant play and Duke's dismal response. Mike Krzyzewski called a timeout.

"We're not going to call any more plays," he told his team. "Let's go down and follow our instincts. Let's be men. And let's play defense."

Duke still trailed 49-38 at the half. Jason Williams made only one of seven field goal attempts in the first half and was held to three points.

Williams regrouped and exploded with 19 points after intermission. His only three-pointer of the night gave Duke its first lead at 73-72 with 6:53 left. Duke pulled away down stretch for 95-84 win, a 33-point turnaround.

After the game Shane Battier, who led all scorers with 25 points, noted, "In our four games each team that won the game was down by double digits. That was in the back of my mind when we were down 20."

"Nobody's 22 points better than Duke," Maryland coach Gary Williams added. "I knew they'd make a run."

This remains the largest deficit any team has ever overcome to win a Final Four contest.

I'M OKAY

Duke freshman guard Chris Duhon collided with Steve Blake late in the Maryland game, suffered a mild concussion, and briefly lost consciousness. The Duke medical staff cleared him to play, but Mike Krzyzewski wanted a second opinion.

He asked Duhon's mother, Vivian Harper, what she thought. She told him that her son could play with two broken legs and two broken arms. Krzyzewski later explained that he didn't want Duhon to go into the title game with memories of the injury but rather with memories of coming back onto the court so he put him back in for the game's closing moments.

RIDING INTO THE SUNSET

Duke met a loaded Arizona team for the 2001 national title. Sophomore Mike Dunleavy broke open a close game with 18 second-half points, and Duke prevailed 82-72.

Not surprisingly, consensus National Player of the Year Shane Battier made repeated big plays down the stretch, ending the game with 18 points, 11 rebounds, six assists, and the Most Outstanding Player Award. The win was Battier's 131st, tying him with Kentucky's Wayne Turner for the most wins in NCAA history.

After the game Battier noted, "It's fitting. It's the perfect ending. All that is left is for me to ride off into the sunset on a white horse.

"I'm a firm believer in guardian angels. A couple of moments down the stretch I believe my two angels were looking after me."

Mike Krzyzewski responded, "Can you do me a favor and leave the guardian angels behind?"

KARMA

Somehow the word karma came up in the postgame press conference. Mike Krzyzewski's take on karma?

"I'm a Polish guy. Is karma a sausage? I'm an inner-city Chicago guy. We don't do karma stuff. I'm going to have to ask Shane to explain this. Wait a second. I think karma may have been the second baseman on my old baseball team back in Chicago."

DUKE AND KENTUCKY AGAIN

Duke and Kentucky have had a number of memorable games in the NCAA Tournament. They don't play often in the regular season. On December 18, 2001, the two clubs met in Madison Square Garden, in a highly anticipated matchup. Led by future NBA regulars Tayshaun Prince and Keith Bogans, Kentucky took a 50-40 lead with 17 minutes left in the game. Mike Krzyzewski benched his entire starting lineup for three minutes, The second team outscored Kentucky 5-4, led by a three-point play by senior Matt Christensen.

"Coach K wasn't looking so much for Xs and Os," Christensen explains. "He wanted us to bring energy and passion into the game."

Following the game, Krzyzewski was asked about having his starters on the bench.

"You're sitting on the bench and you see the kids who practice against you every day, and it's like you're in the ER with the pads on your heart. Boom."

Jason Williams certainly went boom. He scored 23 points in the final 12 minutes to force an overtime, which Duke controlled for a 95-92 win. Williams ended with a career-high 38 points, including seven three-pointers.

DISAPPOINTING SEASON

By most standards the 2002 season was a rousing success for Duke. The Devils lost only four games, captured their fourth consecutive ACC Tournament title, and went into the NCAA Tournament ranked number one in the nation. Juniors Jason Williams, Carlos Boozer, and Mike Dunleavy were all selected first-team All-ACC, the first time that had happened. Williams captured the National Player of the Year awards.

Yet Maryland edged out Duke for first place in the ACC regular season and went on to win the NCAA title. Duke's season ended in the third round of the tournament in an unlikely fashion. Duke led Indiana 30-11 early in the game but lost the lead on missed free throws and poor rebounding.

"Words can't describe how badly we felt," senior Matt Christensen says. "We didn't expect to lose, and suddenly it's over, just over."

REBUILDING

By any rational standard, Duke was in rebuilding mode for 2003. Jason Williams, Carlos Boozer, and Mike Dunleavy passed up their senior seasons for the NBA. But Duke just reloaded.

Senior forward Dahntay Jones made himself into a first-round NBA draft pick, and another talented freshman class, led by guard J.J. Redick and center Shelden Williams, replenished the talent base.

J.J. REDICK

J.J. Redick came down from the Virginia mountains to Duke in the fall of 2002 with the reputation as a great shooter. By the end of his junior year, he was regarded as the best pure shooter in Duke history and one of the best to ever play college basketball.

Some observers are impressed by his form. North Carolina All-American Rashad McCants told *Sports Illustrated*, "I have to be a little cocky about this one, but I think my form is pretty perfect. The only person whose form is a little better is J.J. Redick. He is literally, unbelievably perfect, and mine is behind his."

Some observers were impressed by his range. After Redick scored 33 points against his team in 2005, Wake Forest coach Skip Prosser marveled, "We were playing defense in the 336 area code, and he was shooting from the 919 area code."

Some observers are impressed by his ability to hit shots with defenders hanging all over him. After Redick scored 35 points to help Duke oust North Carolina State in the 2005 ACC Tournament, North Carolina State coach Herb Sendek noted, "None of those shots came with us having our legs crossed and our hands behind our backs. He's a big guard, and he's able to get his shots off with little time or space. He has a lightning-quick release."

Redick articulates the classic shooter's philosophy.

"I'm never surprised by any shot I take. I wouldn't take it if I didn't think it was going in."

NUMBER FIVE

Duke finished second in the 2003 ACC regular season but captured its fifth consecutive ACC Tournament title, extending the record set the previous year. Sophomore guard Daniel Ewing keyed Duke to wins over Virginia and North Carolina with 32 and 19 points respectively. Duke trailed North Carolina State 55-40 with 11:45 left in the title game.

At the timeout, in the words of J.J. Redick, "It was like this. Coach talked, and we listened."

Evidently, Mike Krzyzewski told Redick to make some shots. The precocious freshman outscored State 23-22 down the stretch. Redick and Dahntay Jones scored all of Duke's points in a late 12-0 Duke run that put Duke ahead for good. Redick ended with 30 points, as Duke won 82-77.

"I've probably played this title game 20 to 25 times," Redick said after the game. "The opponent was always different, but I was always playing for Duke."

"He has a gift and knows how to use it," Jones added.

THE BEST EVER

J.J. Redick's shooting accuracy is best displayed at the foul line. Redick ended his career making 91.2 percent of his free throws—third best in NCAA history. Redick established an ACC record in 2004 when he made 54 consecutive free throws. In 2005 Redick missed three of 10 free throws at home against Virginia Tech. Although many college players would kill to make 70 percent of their free throws, this was Redick's worst performance until his senior season.

The incredulous Cameron Crazies chanted to the officials, "Check the rims!"

NO ONE SCORES INSIDE

Shelden Williams is the best shot-blocker in Duke history. The 6-foot-9 center has all of the tools for defensive intimidation—size, quickness, long arms, leaping ability, and timing. But he claims that attitude is the most important part of blocking shots.

"When I throw myself into the game, I find myself in the position to help, to get a block. It's all mental. You have to have the attitude that no one scores inside. No one."

Williams established a school record with 111 blocks in the 2004 season and broke that record with 122 blocks in 2005 and 137 blocks in 2006. In 2005 Williams also became the first player under Mike Krzyzewski to lead the ACC in rebounding, with an average of 11.2 per game and repeated in 2006 with 10.7 per game.

SHERILL ON REDICK

North Carolina State guard Scooter Sherrill made the newspapers in the 2004 season when he made the following comments about J.J. Redick.

"I think he has a little bit of cockiness to him. You see him hit a three, he's running down court hollering, got his hand up like he's gay or something."

Sherrill later apologized but added, "I hope I can get into his head some. That's what I'm trying to do."

Sherrill evidently failed in his task, as Redick scored 48 points in Duke's two games with North Carolina State that season.

CHRIS DUHON

Great players are usually great scorers, at least in the estimation of most fans. Chris Duhon was never a great scorer at Duke. He averaged less than nine points per game over his four years in Durham. But Duhon did all of the things that great point guards do. He finished his Duke career first in minutes played, second in assists, and first in steals.

Duke assistant coach Johnny Dawkins summed up Duhon's multifaceted contributions, "He's a winner. He does what it takes to win. He scores when we need it, he assists when we need it, he plays defense when we need it."

LUOL DENG

Luol Deng had a circuitous route to Duke. He was born in the Sudan. His father, Aldo, was the minister of transportation when a civil war erupted. Aldo Deng opposed the new government and left the country. The Deng family spent time in Egypt before ending up in England. Luol attended prep school in New Jersey, where he became a top player.

Coaches frequently downplay the talents of their newcomers. Not Mike Krzyzewski. Prior to the 2004 season, he discussed Deng.

"Luol is going to be one of the best players—not just on our team, in the conference, in the country. He's that good. Why hide it?"

Chris Duhon agreed.

"It seems like he can jump from the three-point line and lay it up. He uses his body well. He's probably our best inside finisher when it comes to making layups in traffic. He's going to be a guy who does it all for us."

Krzyzewski and Duhon were correct. Deng averaged 15 points per game and was voted Most Valuable Player of the Southeast Regional. Deng went to the NBA after his freshman season, in part to raise awareness of the plight of his countrymen.

SHOWING STRENGTH

Chris Duhon suffered badly bruised ribs in Duke's 2004 ACC Tournament final game, an overtime loss to Maryland. He continued to play his usually fearless game in the NCAA Tournament, diving on the floor, hurling himself into the stands, and drawing charges.

After grabbing 10 defensive rebounds in an NCAA win over Illinois, the 6-foot-1 captain said, "I have to show strength to these guys. I'm their captain and I'm their leader, and I want them to follow my example. If I take my foot off the gas, it gives them the opportunity to take their foot off the gas. Right now I'm putting pedal to the metal."

THE CAPTAIN TAKES OVER

Duke met Xavier in the Southeast Regional title game. Xavier led 30-28 at the half when Chris Duhon had an animated discussion with Luol Deng.

"Just continue to be the guy you've been all year and treat it like a regular game. Don't make the event bigger than the game, just go out and have fun. You don't have the right mindset right now, and you're not just hurting yourself, you're hurting everybody because we need you out there. You're talented enough that if you give it everything, good things are going to happen for us."

Deng had gone one for six from the field in the first half but made six of seven shots after intermission, as Duke came back for a 66-63 win.

After the game Deng said, "At halftime I was really down on myself. I felt like I let my teammates down because I wasn't taking my shots with confidence. I let that affect my defense, where I picked up very bad fouls."

Duhon's defense was equally important.

"Whoever was hot, I put Duhon on him, and they became not hot," Mike Krzyzewski said.

Duhon helped hold Xavier star Romain Sato to two-of-10 shooting.

INTIMIDATED YET?

Nick Horvath came to Duke in the fall of 1998 barely tipping the scales at 200 pounds. By the time he graduated in the spring of 2004, the 6-foot-9 forward's strenuous weightlifting program had bulked him up to 260 pounds. An exceptional student, Horvath applied for a Rhodes Scholarship.

When asked about Horvath's impressive physique, Mike Krzyzewski quipped, "Nick's just trying to intimidate the Rhodes committee."

Horvath didn't get the Rhodes Scholarship but did get a contract to play professional basketball in Australia.

BEST JOB EVER?

At the end of the 2004 season Mike Krzyzewski suggested that his next team could be his most talented. Then rising sophomore Luol Deng and incoming freshman Shaun Livingston surprised the Duke coaching staff by declaring for the NBA draft. This left Duke with only eight recruited players for 2005. Former football player Reggie Love rejoined the team as a 6-foot-4 power forward. This might have worked if everybody had stayed healthy. But five of the top nine players missed extended time with an assortment of injuries and illnesses, and three players had surgery during the season.

Mike Krzyzewski admitted that he took a more hands-on approach to coaching the 2005 team. He worked so hard that he even passed out briefly during a nationally televised game against Georgia Tech.

Afterward, Krzyzewski downplayed the incident.

"I felt like a chump, like somebody hit me with an air punch and I'm out," Krzyzewski said. "I'm on the floor and I'm thinking, 'What an idiot.'"

Duke ended the season with a 27 wins, one over eventual national champion UNC; the school's 15th ACC Tournament championship; and its eighth consecutive trip to the third round of the NCAA Tournament, the third longest such streak in NCAA history. Duke's win over Mississippi State in the NCAA Tournament was Krzyzewski's 66th, passing former North Carolina coach Dean Smith for the top spot in NCAA history. Two wins in the 2006 NCAA Tournament gave Krzyzewski 68 wins.

Noted basketball analyst Billy Packer called the 2005 season "Mike Krzyzewski's best coaching job ever."

DANIEL EWING

How do you develop an ACC-caliber player? One way is to come from a large, competitive family. Growing up in Texas, Daniel Ewing played basketball against his older brothers and struggled.

"They would torture me, beat me down. They wouldn't let me win," he told local media. They'd push me all over the place."

Ewing's father, George, would survey the situation and usually would tell young Daniel to "go back out, but cut out the crying."

J.J. Redick and Shelden Williams received All-America recognition in 2005, but the senior Ewing was the glue of the team. Forced to play point guard when prized recruit Shaun Livingston went directly to the NBA, Ewing led Duke in assists and steals, and averaged 15 points per game.

Mike Krzyzewski praised his consistency.

"Daniel works hard and is remarkably steady. He has some outstanding games but never bad games."

NEVER DONE IT BEFORE

Duke has had some great buzzer beaters in its history, but few equal the one on December 4, 2005. Duke trailed Virginia Tech at home 75-74 and had to go the length of the floor with only 1.6 seconds left. Following a time-out, Josh McRoberts threw a pass just past midcourt. Sean Dockery caught it, turned, and launched a desperation 40-footer. Dockery said, "When I let go of the ball, it looked like one of J.J.'s shots that was rotating just perfect and looked like it was going in. It felt like it was in the air forever." Dockery's shot swished through the nets, giving Duke an improbable 77-75 win. Dockery noted, "I'm the guy that never makes that shot in practice. That was my first one, so I'm now like 1-for-30. You dream about shots like that when you are playing in the backyard or in your room."

KEEPING 'EM LOOSE

Coming out of high school, Lee Melchionni—the son of former Duke star Gary Melchionni—wasn't as highly regarded as Duke classmates J.J. Redick, Shelden Williams, Sean Dockery, or Shavlik Randolph. But the forward bided his time and became a valuable member of the rotation in his junior and senior seasons. He also was the team cutup, always willing and able to break up tension with a quip or a practical joke.

In one game Duke was warming up when Melchionni noticed a sign in the stands that read, "Call Shelden Williams at [phone number]! Tell him he's ugly!" Melchionni and Williams broke up.

Only later did Williams learn that Melchionni had planted the number and that it wasn't Williams' number but rather the number of one of Melchionni's friends from Pennsylvania, a friend whose voice mail was soon inundated with phone calls. After the 2006 season, Melchionni quipped, "J.J. and Shelden will both be lottery picks, and I couldn't be more excited for them. Maybe they'll lend me some money."

LET HIM HAVE HIS POINTS?

J.J. Redick had one of the greatest individual seasons in ACC history in 2005-2006, averaging a school record 26.8 points per game and breaking numerous ACC and NCAA records. One sportswriter suggested to Florida State coach Leonard Hamilton that he simply concede a certain number of points to Redick. The incredulous Hamilton responded, "If you let him have his points, he might score 70. I'm not real sure I want to play that Russian roulette. That's your theory. I think you need to try to get [yourself] a team and try it out, but I don't think you should try it with Redick."

SUPERSTAR COACH

Johnny Dawkins had an unusual vantage point for Redick's assault on the record books. The Duke assistant was not only courtside, he also was helping Redick surpass his Duke career record. Head coach Mike Krzyzewski noted Dawkins' unique contributions to Redick. "The thing that Johnny does that none of us on the staff can do is identify with that great player because he was that great player. I've coached guys like that, but I've never been that guy. J.J.'s fortunate to have him here."

DICKIE HEMRIC

Fifty years after former Wake Forest star Dickie Hemric retired from basketball, he gained the respect of a new generation of fans as Redick chased his ACC career scoring record. Hemric was consistently gracious, telling a national television audience, "I knew it would happen sooner or later. Better a Blue Devil than a Tar Heel."

THE LANDLORD

Shelden Williams acquired the nickname "The Landlord" in high school because of his defensive dominance in the paint. Opponents would need to pay the landlord to even visit. Quiet and reserved by nature, he was overshadowed much of his career by more volatile personalities and in 2006 by J.J. Redick's relentless pursuit of several high-profile records. Yet Williams passed Mike Gminski to become Duke's career leader in rebounds and blocked shots and was named national Defensive Player of the Year in 2005 and 2006. On January 11, 2006, Williams recorded 19 points, 11 rebounds, and 10 blocks in a win over Maryland, only the third triple-double in school history. Mike Krzyzewski says of Williams, "He's great, in every sense of the word. We're so lucky to have him. He's going to go down as one of the great players in this conference."

IT JUST HAPPENED

In an extraordinary 10-day run in late February 2006, J.J. Redick broke Curtis Staples' NCAA record for career three-point shots, Johnny Dawkins' Duke career scoring record, and Dickie Hemric's ACC career scoring record. It was an exhilarating, exhausting, and sometimes distracting run that attracted extensive national media attention. After breaking Hemric's record, Redick noted, "I never really set out to do it or concentrate on it. It just kind of came about with the season I was having."

Not everyone was as sanguine as Redick about his accomplishments. He was named ACC Player of the Year for the second time, captured all of the national Player of the Year awards (sharing one with Gonzaga's Adam Morrison) and won the Sullivan Award as America's top amateur athlete in any sport. Redick ended his Duke career with 457 made three-point shots and 2,769 points.

EPILOGUE

The 2005-06 season was the 101st in Duke history. Duke started its second century as strongly as it ended its first. Duke was ranked No. 1 much of the season, captured the preseason NIT Tournament, finished first in the ACC regular season, won its record 16th ACC Tournament, and advanced to the Sweet Sixteen of the NCAA

Tournament for the ninth consecutive season. Mike Krzyzewski has won 680 games at Duke, while the school ranks fourth in NCAA wins, third in NCAA Tournament wins, and first in NCAA winning percentage.

Chapter 7

BACK TO
THE TOP

MCCLURE FOR THE WIN

You never can tell who's going to be a hero. David McClure was a defensive-oriented role player for Duke from 2005–2009. He scored a modest 278 points in 124 games at Duke.

But in 2007, McClure provided one of the most dramatic baskets imaginable. Duke was at home against Clemson and the Tigers had just tied the game 66–66, with 4.4 seconds remaining.

Duke called time-out to set up the potential game-winner. The plan was for Josh McRoberts to inbound to Jon Scheyer. McClure would set a screen for Scheyer, who would either take the final shot himself or find DeMarcus Nelson in the corner.

Instead McClure broke free down the middle, took Scheyer's pass in full stride, and laid the ball in the basket as two defenders closed on him and the clock struck zero.

"We were trying to keep everybody composed," McClure said after the game. "We were just trying to set something up to give us a chance to win the game. It was actually designed for Jon to curl down here and get a little run towards the basket. They played really good defense on it. It broke down for a second because they were scattered all over the place and I happened to get open. You can't even explain how it feels. I couldn't help it. I started jumping around and about a second later, I got hit by the rest of the team and we all went down."

TAKE THAT, DAD

A father and son playing hoops together is practically a staple of American culture, and finally beating the old man is a rite of passage. But that victory undoubtedly means more when the old man played thirteen years in the NBA.

"My dad's about 6'1"," Gerald Henderson, Jr. says. "He could jump a little bit, but on a different level. He could shoot, though, probably a little better than me. My dad's pretty smart. Once I got to the point where I could beat him, he stopped playing me."

That point was the seventh grade.

THROWN TO THE WOLVES

Mike Krzyzewski likes talking about bridge classes. The quartet of freshmen who arrived at Duke for the 2006–07 season certainly qualifies. By Duke standards, 2007 was a disappointing season; a 22–11 record and first-round losses in both the ACC and NCAA Tournaments.

Youth was a big issue with this team. A series of early NBA entries left Duke with no recruited seniors and only a single recruited junior, wing DeMarcus Nelson. Freshmen Jon Scheyer, Gerald Henderson, Lance Thomas, and Brian Zoubek were all thrust into major roles.

"They were thrown to the wolves," Mike Krzyzewski recalled. "It was our youngest team in the history of Duke basketball, and they didn't have juniors and seniors to walk them through things. Their class is believers. They helped get our culture back. They know what it is not to have anybody. They helped build a championship."

BACK ON TRACK

The first championship was the 2009 ACC Tournament title. Krzyzewski moved junior Scheyer to the point midway through the season, after Greg Paulus and Nolan Smith struggled at the position. After Duke captured the ACC Tournament that year, Krzyzewski dissected the move. "I knew he would handle it. He's such a good player that, placed with that level of responsibility, he's someone who is really good and will show you even better things. What I'm seeing is magnificent play. He's done such a good job because he values the ball."

Krzyzewski added that Duke wasn't going to make highlight reels of Scheyer leading the fast break. That's okay with Scheyer. "It's not like I walk out there and teams are all of a sudden scared to go up against me."

WHAT KEEPS ME GOING

Following Duke's win over Florida State in the 2009 ACC Tournament title game, Mike Krzyzewski was asked what kept him motivated. His answer says a lot about him. "The person doing it has to have different layers of satisfaction. I'm so happy right now experiencing it with these guys. I'm 62 and I'm almost three times as old as these guys. But I feel like we're connected. What they're feeling, I think I feel it a lot. It's not numbers, it's the experience of doing it with quality people."

NOLAN GETS READY

It's said that champions are made in the off-season. Nolan Smith, averaging around seven points per game, struggled with injuries and inconsistency his first two seasons at Duke.

Back to the woodshed. "I knew I was better than that. I worked on my game and on my body. I got stronger, I got quicker, I got in the best condition of my life. I worked on my ball-handling, my three-point shooting, my mid-range game. I played in every pick-up game I could find."

Mission accomplished. Smith averaged 17 points per game as a junior in 2010, and led the ACC with 20.6 points per game as ACC Player of the Year in 2011.

NOT GOING TO HAPPEN AGAIN

Duke's 2007 team started 18–3 before losing eight of their final 12 games. When the 2010 team wobbled in the middle of the season with decisive road losses to North Carolina State and Georgetown, seniors Jon Scheyer, Brian Zoubek, and Lance Thomas made sure it wouldn't happen again.

"They described how you never want to go there," Miles Plumlee says. "They had been there and they wouldn't let it happen again. They took ownership of the team and wouldn't let it fall apart."

Ryan Kelly agrees. "It started with our seniors. They had been through a lot. Their freshman year was a huge disappointment, in Duke basketball's eyes, the way they ended the season. They had to go through a lot where they had to grow and become men. They had an unbelievable ability to pass that on to the younger guys. Kyle and Nolan really grew from that. Things weren't perfect. Bumps in the road happen. To be able to take those things, learn from them and just become better from them. Those guys did that so well. They pushed the rest of the team to the point that it made them better. In doing that, they became really good players. That sense of leadership made you feel close to them. It just builds unity."

EPIC BEAT DOWN

Duke and North Carolina have played some of the most compelling, down-to-the-wire games in college basketball history.

March 6, 2010, wasn't one of them. It was senior day for Scheyer, Zoubek, and Thomas. Duke led 53–26 at the half and cruised to an 82–50 win, Duke's biggest victory margin over Carolina since 1964.

Scheyer scored 20 points in his final game in Cameron. "You never go into a game thinking you're going to blow somebody out by 30. But once we get a lead like that, we really want to have a killer instinct and put them away. I thought we never let off the gas. Nolan, Kyle and I told each other before the game that we needed to have a game where the three of us start, every one of us start playing better. I thought that happened tonight, and it was a step in the right direction."

The right direction would end with an NCAA title a month later.

BIGGEST FREE THROW EVER

Brian Zoubek went to the free throw line with 3.6 seconds remaining in the 2010 National Championship game and Duke up by a single point. What was going through his mind? "Fifty percent is thinking, 'This is what I've been dreaming of doing my entire life.' Fifty percent, I'm crapping my pants."

YES, I SAW IT

Zoubek made the first foul shot but missed the second on purpose, since Butler was out of timeouts. Butler star Gordon Hayward barely missed a mid-court heave that would have won the game for his team. Kyle Singler was guarding Hayward until he was leveled by a Butler screen. Lying on the court, Singler had a great view of the near miss. "When I got screened, I kind of twisted the right way to see the ball. I saw the ball bounce off the backboard and hit the rim. It looked good. It was just one of those things where you're wishing and hoping that it won't go in."

SENIORS REFLECT ON TITLE

Kyle Singler was named Most Outstanding Player of the 2010 Final Four, while fellow junior Nolan Smith also played superbly.

But the title may have meant the most to Jon Scheyer, Lance Thomas, and Brian Zoubek, the three seniors who had fought through the 11-loss season of their freshman year.

Their thoughts?

Jon Scheyer: "I don't think many people can say they went out winning a national championship. I don't think any of us could have predicted the four years we had here."

Lance Thomas: "It means the world to us, especially our senior class. To come in and get knocked out of this tournament in our first game and to have to live with that for the rest of our lives and the extra years after that, our sophomore and junior year, just not getting the success we want and to leave champions. We maxed out our season."

Brian Zoubek: "It's been an absolute progression. You can see the difference every single year. To end it like this, is undescribable. I really don't think our seniors could have predicted this kind of success through our career, just based on how our freshman year went. It just proves that if you keep with it, keep your head down, keep working at it, good things will come if you put in the work."

THE FAMILY BUSINESS

Duke has had numerous players who have successful athletes in their family.

That certainly applies to Seth Curry, whose father, Dell, played 16 seasons in the NBA and whose brother, Stephen, is an NBA star with Golden State.

Seth says that his father and brother are invaluable resources. "I talk to my father and Stephen pretty often. We're a basketball family. That's what we talk about. They're honest with me. They don't just tell me what I want to hear. There's lots of wisdom there. I look at the game in a different way than other players do. I know tricks of the trade just because of being around the game so much."

WHAT MIGHT HAVE BEEN

Kyrie Irving is one of the great what-might-have-beens in Duke basketball history. The number one pick in the 2011 NBA draft, Irving played eight games before injuring a toe against Butler. Those games included a 31-point performance against powerful Michigan State.

Irving's injury kept him out until the NCAA Tournament, by which point Duke had reconfigured its team dynamics. Irving played well upon his return, but Duke lost to Arizona in the Sweet Sixteen.

Mike Krzyzewski discussed how Irving's absence impacted Duke. "If Kyrie was healthy the whole year, the perimeter we would have would be him, Nolan, and Kyle for the entire season, which would be a formidable perimeter. What happened is we practiced for two months, played eight games playing a certain way, and when you have a strength that's that strong on the perimeter you don't have to show your weaknesses, and as soon as he went down, our weaknesses were exposed, and we didn't have the two months before to correct those weaknesses. So we basically started our preseason in the middle of December."

WINNING CHAMPIONSHIPS

Duke has had great success in early-season tournaments, including a perfect five Maui Classic championships in five tries. Duke assistant coaches Steve Wojciechowski and Chris Collins both played on Maui title teams and coached them.

They agree that winning early sets the tone for winning later. "Duke expects to win championships and what better time to start than November?" Wojciechowski says. "These tournaments can give you a true picture of where you're at. It's invaluable in that respect. It's the first time your group can pursue a championship. We're there to play basketball. The way to build fond memories is to win."

Chris Collins agrees, "If you want to be a champion, win a championship. That can't be taken away."

BROTHERLY LOVE

Brothers Miles and Mason Plumlee grew up in Warsaw, Indiana. Miles is 18 months older. Both parents played college basketball, so playing hoops is part of the family DNA.

But forget being brothers-in-arms. "We lived in a sub-division, with a goal in the driveway," Miles recalls. "We played every day. That's all we had to do. Mason and I really went after it. It got pretty intense, pretty physical. It reached the point that we couldn't play against each other unless our Dad came out and called fouls. We got past that. But it helped both of us. Where else were we going to find someone that big to play against?"

THE ULTIMATE ROAD TRIP

Road trips are a great way to bond. But what about Duke's around-the-world road trip during the summer of 2011? Three games in China, one in Dubai, and lots of time on airplanes.

Miles Plumlee recalls a side trip to the Great Wall of China. "It was early in the morning. We could have taken a gondola to the top. But we wanted to climb to the top. How tough could that be? Well, it was really, really hard. We had no idea how many steps we would have to climb. It seemed like it took an hour. It was pretty intense. Everybody made it but some guys were throwing up and I was close. I'm not sure I want to bond like that again."

Ryan Kelly remembers the climb but more vividly remembers the long plane rides getting there. "The feeling of getting off that plane and going to the game. The game was pretty much right away. You were so happy to get off that plane and you want to play basketball just to get moving but you can't move. You just try to sleep as long as you can. But that's something you're willing to sacrifice for the trip. How many people get the chance to see China through the eyes of Duke basketball? It was awesome."

Duke won all three games in China and its only game in Dubai.

COACH K AT THE TOP

The United States Military Academy, a.k.a. Army, has never had a men's basketball team advance to the NCAA Tournament. But the two winningest coaches in men's Division 1 history began their head-coaching careers at Army before moving on the bigger things.

So when Mike Krzyzewski moved past his former coach Bobby Knight to take over the top spot, Coach K's thoughts turned to his mentor.

"I just told Coach I love him. I wouldn't be in this position without him. It's a moment shared. I know he's very proud, and I'm very proud to have been somebody who's worked under him and studied him and tried to be like him. I'm not sure how many people tell him they love him, but I love him for what he's done for me, and I thanked him. He said, 'Boy, you've done pretty good for a kid who couldn't shoot.' I think that means he loves me too. At least that's how I'm taking that."

AUSTIN RIVERS' DAGGER

The Duke-North Carolina rivalry has produced some stunning finishes. But few could match what happened in Chapel Hill February 8, 2012, when Duke overcame a 10-point deficit in the final two minutes.

Freshman Austin Rivers buried a 3-pointer at the buzzer to give Duke the 75–74 win, calmly shooting over seven-footer Tyler Zeller.

Rivers tells how it happened. "I was supposed to go to the lane and get fouled. I didn't plan on shooting a three. I saw Zeller was on me and if he had crowded me, I would have drove. You just have to read things. Zeller stepped off a little bit thinking I was going to drive. I gave him my jab step, and I was hitting him with hesitation. The shot was there, and I just took it. I just shot the ball with confidence. I saw it on target, and my heart dropped for a second because you don't know. That shot was the slowest shot I've ever seen. I swear the ball was in the air for like five minutes. It looked good, and I was like, 'Please go in.' When it went through the hoop, my heart jumped and I saw the buzzer ring. I just ran across half-court and turned around and I saw my team running at me. It was the best feeling I've ever had in my life. It was amazing."

Teammate Seth Curry had a great view of the shot. "He kept dribbling and dribbling, and I wasn't sure if he saw the clock or not, so I was like, 'Go! Go!' I thought time was going to run out, but he put it up at the last second and knocked it down."

ONE DAY AT A TIME

Mike Krzyzewski says staying in the moment has allowed him to coach for almost forty years. "I coach every game like it's my first game, and my mom and dad, the neighborhood I came from believed that. The next game, the next thing you do is the important thing you do. How does it turn out? You know, you don't look too far ahead, and you definitely don't look back; but you really focus on now, and that's the way I've enjoyed coaching and it's turned out well."